LIGHTNING ON THE HORIZON

Trauma and the Human Condition IV

ANNGWYN ST. JUST

Also by Anngwyn St. Just

*At Paradigm's Edge: Trauma and the Human Condition III,
Createspace USA 2014*

*Waking to the Sound of Thunder: Trauma and the Human
Condition II, Createspace USA 2013*

*Trauma and the Human Condition: Notes from the Internaional
Field, Createspace USA 2012*

*Trauma: Time Space and Fractals : A Systemic Perspective on
Individual, Social and Global Trauma, Createspace USA 2012*

*A Question of Balance: A Systemic Approach to Understanding
and Resolving Trauma, Createspace USA 2009*

*Relative Balance in an Unstable World: A Search for New
Models for Trauma Education and Recovery, Carl-Auer Verlag,
Heidelberg, Germany 2006*

In Translation:

*Trauma: Tiempo, espacio y fractales
Editorial Alma Lepik, Buenos Aires, Argentina, 2012*

*Trauma: Una cuestion de equilibrio: Un abordaje sistemico para la
comprension y resolucion,
Editorial Alma Lepik, Buenos Aires, Argentina, 2011*

*Equilibrio relativo en un mundo inestable: Una investigacion sobre
Educacion de Trauma y Recuperacion, 2nd ed.
Editorial Alma Lepik, Buenos Aires, Argentina, 2011*

*Sociales Trauma: Balance finden in einer unsicheren Welt
Kösel Verlag/Random House, München, Deutchland, 2005*

Table of Contents

November:

December:

Dedication

This latest contribution to the study of Trauma and the Human Condition is dedicated to my nearly forgotten and almost lost ancestor, Leah Maria Van Riper. I never knew her, of course, because she was long gone before I was born and I knew about her existence only through her Dutch Reform Bible, which always had a revered place upon a small table in my Grandmother's parlor. In those days in her antique household, there was a living room for family and a separate parlor for receiving guests. Of course, as a child I was curious, but still there was no information forthcoming; and none of my close relatives were especially religious.

Years later, when I brought this unresolved connection to my husband, who speaks fluent Dutch; he speculated that Leah Maria's family were from the North-Holland town of De Rijp. So when we were in Holland we ventured out to this beautiful place, where I felt, at least temporarily, and transiently, some strange sense of home - and gratitude for all who still reside there.

We actually found the Dutch Reform Church to which her ancestors belonged, before they set sail for New Amsterdam; which eventually became New York.

I am especially grateful to my cousin Christopher John Schopfer for all of his diligent genealogical research.

Under a Thunderhead

Under a thunderhead
in a suddenly darkened field,
straight backed against a stone,
I wait.
like a hunted thing
charmed into paralysis
by a great predator growling
distantly igniting the silver lining,
blowing the fuse
of everything I was promised
as the trees fill
their great sails
and the ridge line fails-
That great wall breached!
Under that great thunderhead
I am still here
as the temperature drops five degrees
because, not I
but something being born in me,
that has storm tested wings,
wants to stay no matter what,
instead of dashing for the house

to watch from inside
as I have watched,
how many storms?
unhinge this gentle place,
trap the stillborn moment,
in that coppery light
while the ever-breaking wave,
the wind,
drags that weighted curtain,
of the rain we always say we need.

Gary Lindorff   (August 2105)

Introduction

"We are now a global community and as responsible global citizens we need to be aware of what is happening in the world... Nothing is somewhere else". (Llewellyn Vaughn-Lee)

"The realization that every act, every word, every thought of ours not only influences our environment but for some mysterious reason forms an important part of the Universe, fits into it, as if by necessity, so to say, in the very moment we do or say or think it, is an overwhelming or even shattering experience.... If we know this deeply and absolutely...if this realization becomes permanently engraved on our hearts, and in our minds, how carefully we would act and speak and think". (Irina Tweedy).

"Our beliefs become our thoughts, our thoughts become our words, our words become our habits, which then become our values, and then our values become our destiny". (Mahatma Gandhi, 1868- 1948)

This current volume is the fourth in a series of **Trauma and the Human Condition** "blooks" (blogs + books) which are essentially a compendium of monthly online blogs, offered during the calendar year through the auspices of the **Western Institute for Social**

Research in Berkeley, California, since 2011. While most entries within this year's collection have been posted throughout the year, some have been expanded and updated, as new information has become available. Given that I am a systemically oriented social traumatologist, my overall focus has remained, for the most part, upon issues having to do with social and global traumas which contribute to the ongoing process of increasingly rapid social change, due to globalization and the Internet; in conjunction with transnational, corporate and state-sponsored communication and surveillance technologies.

We now find ourselves living in an era which futurist Alvin Toffler defined as "future shock", a psychological state experienced by individuals and societies undergoing "too much change in too short a period of time". Toffler's vision, later released as a documentary narrated by Orson Wells **(Future Shock,** 1970), also included the term "information overload" which, to my mind might also include a reality of too much information unfortunately combined with a serious shortage of wisdom.

Now well into my seventh decade, I have been witness to our white-knuckle transition from a rather bland, post-war, Eisenhower-era republic, (throughout the exciting and turbulent sixties), to our truly spectacular Space-Age global empire. In retrospect, I would venture that Toffler vastly underestimated our biological capacities for adaptation and change, although we have a cadre of fiercely loyal and patriotic citizens who remain deeply troubled by some of these changes; especially those involving the ever increasing militarism of our 21st century America. As those who study history know, terror, intimidation and violence have provided an oppressive, conglomerate glue which has held all of the great empires together; while simultaneously incubating and eventually germinating, the seeds of their eventual downfall and destruction.

Among those concerned about the implications and potential consequences of our inevitably impending, collective national destiny, Chris Hedges, (Harvard trained theologian, foreign correspondent and best-selling author of **Empire of Delusion: The End of Literacy and The Triumph of Spectacle);** cautions that we have engaged in despicably theatrical "shock and awe". Among these atrocities we have launched aerial bombardments, drone and missile attacks, artillery and mortar strikes, targeted assassinations, overt and covert massacres, the detention of tens of thousands, death-squad killings, torture, pervasive surveillance, extraordinary renditions, (kidnap and torture), curfews, cynical propaganda, and the loss of civil liberties.

Much of this horror has been enabled by bought-and-paid for, black-mailed and otherwise comprised and therefore pliant, political-puppets willing to provide any necessary grist for our for-profit, proxy resource wars. Following any of this on mainstream news; it is presented as something like an infomercial for the wonders of the elite, trans-national "powers that be". Corporate-controlled news outlets proudly display their newly-minted weapons promoted by the seemingly endless financial resources of the military-industrial-media, complex.
(Chris Hedges, commondreams, January 1, 2016)

In all fairness, Toffler, while focusing on the psycho-social aspects of rapid change, may not have foreseen the darker political sides of his vision; he did however offer a useful definition of sanity as, "the ability to tell the real from the unreal". Now however, within our increasingly prevalent, matrix-generated consensus-reality, we are in need of a new definition. This, it seems, has become an ongoing challenge, given the fact that, as journalist Jon Rappaport points out; a criminal class has been inventing reality for us and they have been doing this since the dawn of time.

In modern times, master blueprints of social engineering have been updated by cultural critics George Orwell, and Aldous Huxley. In light of our most recent events I felt that January's "Dystopian Convergence: Big Brother's Brave New World" provided an overall context for many, if not most, of the subsequent pieces throughout the year. While speaking truth to power may be the preferred mode of many of our awake and aware, I find that humor also has its place, and there are times when humor might serve just as well as in "Clickbait Headlines", "America's War on Halloween" and finally the squirrel infested "Year of Fear". Although this year's topics appear in a linear sequence, some may be of more interest than others and need not be read in any particular order.

Anngwyn St. Just, January 1st, 2016

JANUARY

Dystopian Convergence:
Big Brother's Brave New World

"When the tyrant has disposed of foreign enemies by conquest or treaty, and there is nothing to fear from them, then he is always stirring up some war or other, in order that people may require a leader". (Plato, **The Republic,** c. 380 B.C.)

"Never attempt to win by force what can be won by deception". (Niccolo Machiavelli, The Prince, 1513)

"*A criminal class is busy inventing reality for us. They've been doing it since the dawn of time".* (Jon Rappaport, rense.com)

"Folly is perennial, yet the human race has survived". (Bertrand Russell, Philosopher, 1873-1970)

January, this first month of our new year has been traditionally associated with the ancient Roman deity Janus, usually depicted with two faces. One face sees deep into the past while the other sees far into the future. (Gary Forsythe, **Time in Roman Religions**, 2012). January is also a traditional month for issuing future predictions; and various astrologers, psychics and other soothsayers, political-prognosticators and various purveyors of economic and financial futures; show up around various media outlets with a usually predictable collection of likely scenarios for the coming year.

Plainspoken **Trends Journal** founder, Gerald Celente, ranks among the most credible forecasters, with an impressive track record for accuracy. While admitting to occasional hunches, he denies that any so-called *woo-woo* elements play any role within his common-sense predictions. Celente maintains that his is a very straightforward method since, "current events predict future trends". While I don't disagree, I would also suggest that the handwriting for humanity has long since been on the wall; at least as far back as fourth century BCE Plato's, **The Republic;** together with Machiavelli's Renaissance classic **The Prince.**

In recent times, master blueprints for social engineering were updated and clearly set forth during the twentieth century by Aldous Huxley and George Orwell. These British social critics and literary titans knew each other from a time when Huxley was Orwell's professor of French at Eton. In later life they often corresponded and exchanged ideas as well as published works. To this day they are often paired for compare-and-contrast assignments in English and (other literature) and political-science classes. Among online and other pundits they are often framed as oppositional, in articles such as "Orwell Versus Huxley: Who Are You Behind?" (Laureen Feeny, billmoyers.com, April27,2012).

While their differences are interesting enough, more important is the fact that both essentially took different routes to the same destination. Both Orwell and Huxley, mutually influenced by H.G. Wells, shared a futuristic vision and clear warning about social-engineering agendas designed to implement and carry out nothing less than an absolute, totalitarian, control and oppression of the independent human spirit.

George Orwell is the pen-name for Eric Blair and **1984** was a permutation of 1948, the year during which his novel was written. While many of his dystopian predictions did not manifest by his designated date, here in the 21st century many of his state-sanctioned formulas for fear, control, universal surveillance and state-staged false-flag and controlled media-theatrics; seem uncomfortably familiar. Orwell evoked a New World Order which is divided between three superpowers: Oceania, Eastasia, and Eurasia, which continue to rotate through an ongoing series of alliances and hostilities designed to create a planet-wide, new-normal of endless, un-winnable wars. Populations are divided into political castes, headed by a ruling minority of the now-familiar one percent; whose only goal is to obtain and maintain power; forever.

The projected face of these global controllers appears in Orwell's, possibly fictional, media-constructed, omnipotent, "Big Brother"; who is unquestionably served by an all-pervasive surveillance-network, aided by omnipresent tele-screens. Therefore, any renegade thinkers who attempt to assert any individuality, are quickly discovered and subjected to trauma-based mind-control; tortured and brainwashed into compliance.

While more or less of the many versions of a Big Brother figure have appeared in fiction, here in the USA his recent incarnation in the form of Janet Napolitano's "Big Sis", has not been all that well received. She has since stepped down from her position as Head of the Department of Homeland Security, in order to serve the next agenda in the military/industrial/nuclear/academic complex; within the widespread University of California educational systems.

In **1984**, education is dictated by an omnipotent state, and curriculums are mandated by their "Ministry of Truth", whose task it is to re-write history and edit all school textbooks, according to an official agenda; and to permanently disappear any authentic documents with contrary information into a deep memory hole of oblivion.

With a similar agenda already in place, within this country, it is no small wonder that increasing numbers of concerned parents are now choosing to Home School, find private educational resources; or campaign against government mandated, "No Child

Left Behind", robotic, dumbed-down, test-taking agendas, created and promoted by various members of the Bush family cabal. Educators within Orwell's caste system are to be found among the outer 13 percent of devoted minions of the controlling elite; as we might now observe in the military-industrial takeover of our once magnificent, private and public universities. Orwell's novels, including his anti-fascist/anti-communist, **Animal Farm,** written in 1945, carry a similar message: All dictatorships are basically the same.

In our post 9/11 surveillance-state, supposedly protected by the euphemistically-titled Department of Homeland Security, privacy has nearly ceased to exist due to their never-ending, un-winnable wars on terror, drugs and so on. Our Mockingbird media even went so far as to postulate an extremely urgent, "War on Christmas". Iconic Orwellian terms once considered fictional such as "Big Brother" have now become a familiar reality, as well as "group-think", "thought police", "thought crime", "pre-crime", "boots in your face"; and newspeak and cognitive-dissonance slogans reminiscent of **1984**'s "War is

Peace", "Ignorance is Strength", "Freedom is Slavery" and the infamous Nazi: *Arbeit Macht Frei.* Orwell's 85 percent population of "proles" are kept stupid and malleable through the use of alcohol, moronic epithets, pornography and gambling through a national lottery which nobody ever wins.

National solidarity and loyalty to Big Brother and The Party is generated by a ritualized two minutes of "hate speak", directed against the possibly non-existent Emmanuel Goldstein, "the enemy of us all". Goldstein's face appears everywhere to remind the terrified populace of an ongoing threat from this "enemy of the state". This fictional scenario is also uncomfortably familiar to those us who remember the ubiquitous, so called Osama Bin Laden tapes, demonizing this former US ally, as the architect of 9/11, who, credible sources report, died of kidney failure sometime during 2001. Meanwhile, another former ally was soon to be seen all over our mediam, as Saddam Hussein was announced as "another Hitler", hoarding "weapons of mass destruction".

Most recently, our modern day "hate speak" efforts have been directed toward a shadowy ISIS, Al-CIA-da offshoot, Muslim terrorist group, of dubious origin, who appeared suspiciously well-armed and seemingly out of nowhere. If you are still unclear as to the reality and function of hate-speak, you might tune into the Fox News propaganda channel or almost any extreme right wing talk-radio show, or web site ... and there are many from which to choose. These belligerently patriotic sites, not shy about advocating violence, now provide a venue where frightened citizens can all get together and feel really good and oh, so righteously connected through mutual terror and loathing of the latest state determined "Emmanuel Goldstein/other".

Orwell's novel concludes with a reality from which there is no escape; from a pervasive militaristic oppression and deceitful multi-media matrix which controls through promotion of heightened fear and pain.

In **Brave New World,** Huxley's equally oppressive, scientific dystopia controls through desire, pleasure and distraction while advanced technology provides an excess of material comfort along with subliminal suggestions, mass-marketing hypnosis and mind control. Set in London in the year 2540, Huxley's dark social satire takes place in a globalist World State, where unhappiness and emotion are managed through drugs. While not opposed to psychedelics, Huxley foresaw the pervasive influence of Big Pharma in social engineering through his depiction of the hallucinogen Soma, which relieved users of any discomforts presented by anything resembling reality.

In the interest of eugenics, recreational sex, extending to the point of hedonistic nihilism, while encouraged, is disconnected from reproduction; practically non-existent family life is considered pornographic while human pregnancies are condemned as obscene. As a result of strict population control, offspring are produced in factory-farm hatcheries. Genetically engineered clones and designer babies are artificially gestated in ecto-genesis devices which produce five chemically and hormonally determined casts: intelligent Alphas, only slightly less gifted Beta minions, and then Gammas, Deltas, and unfortunate Epsilons; artificially bred according to their designated social status and assigned roles within a carefully controlled, absolutely immutable, social hierarchy. The only options for escape were insanity or self-imposed exile to an off- the-grid existence among "savages" and primitive living conditions.

Aldous Huxley was deeply familiar with the desired practices and goals in the evolving science of eugenics, now called trans-humanism, through the work of his brother Julian Huxley (1887-1975), an evolutionary biologist who served for many years as President of the British Eugenics Society, now called the Galton Institute. This group advocated restricting reproduction to healthy, "fit", individuals and forbidding any breeding among "unfit" individuals. Many of their ideas provided ample inspiration for the Nazi Third Reich's policies of "racial hygiene".

It is important to bear in mind, not only the disastrous application of these eugenics and genetic theories and their potential for social engineering and genocide, but the reality that many of their so called "unfit" actually have what we may understand as "different minds"   bodies and abilities. For example, Steven Hawking, Helen Keller, Alan Turing, Albert Einstein, Vincent Van Gogh, Ludwig van Beethoven; as well as untold numbers of extraordinary, brilliant and talented others.

In 1958 Huxley updated his thoughts in, **Brave New World Re-Visited,** which concluded that our world was moving toward his dystopian vision much faster than he had originally predicted. His concerns included both overpopulation and population control as well as the social effects of psychoactive drugs, hedonistic sex, and the use of subliminal suggestion through advertising, political propaganda and other mass-marketing, multi-layered, mega-media agendas; using any form of mind control to create a consensual reality.

In **Amusing Ourselves to Death** (1985), the late Neil Postman published a lively polemic restating Huxley's warning of a consumer-driven society that leads to a culture of burlesque. Not only will people be laughing instead of thinking, but they won't know what they are laughing about and why they had stopped thinking. In an age of advancing technology, spiritual devastation is more likely to come from telegenic leaders and media "personalities" who seduce with a perpetual round of smooth lies, gratuitous violence, disaster-porn and entertaining irrelevant trivia. It could be said that we now live in an age of smart phones and dumb people; increasingly unable to distinguish between actual and virtual reality; a task rendered all the more difficult with an advent of green-screens, Photoshop and computer generated imagery.

In our modern dystopias it is not difficult to recognize elements from both Orwell's and Huxley's prescient visions. Here in America, for example we have an all- pervasive surveillance system, which may well be global; to the extent that personal privacy is nearly impossible, with "boots in the face" law enforcement which can arrest, brutalize and kill with impunity. Nevertheless, we have also come to love, depend upon and even become addicted to our electronic leashes; TVs, DVDs, cell phones, computers, email, Twitter accounts, Facebook "friends" and other options for shallow exchanges of pseudo-connectivity.

We may recognize other aspects of ourselves and our current situation in similar dystopian novels such as Hungarian born English novelist, Arthur Koestler's, **Darkness at Noon** (1940), Ray Bradbury's **Fahrenheit 451** (1953), Philip K. Dick's **Do Android's Dream of Electronic Sheep?;** later recreated in the 1958 film **Blade Runner.** We have an abundance of provocative examples in many other films as well, such as my favorite, the now classic American-Australian: **The Matrix** (1999), which contains a number of cinematic and literary works and concepts from mythology, religion, and philosophy; including Plato's **Allegory of the Cave**, whose prisoners mistake firelight and flickering shadows projected upon their walls, as reality. While we are long out of our caves, how many of us can distinguish the soft glow of our flickering screens from reality?

Clickbait Headlines

"It used to be that everyone was entitled to their own opinions, but not their own facts. But that's not the case anymore... Keep your 'facts', I'm going with the truth". (Stephen Colbert)

"As long as people believe in absurdities, they will continue to commit atrocities". (Voltaire)

Some people will believe anything, especially if it appears in some mainstream news outlet. Never mind the fact that 90% of the media in this country is owned and controlled by just six corporations. As a result, we are bombarded with an ongoing blend of state sponsored propaganda, celebrity-gossip infotainment, violence and disaster-porn, cover-ups, half-truths and outright lies. As a recent case in point, we might consider the multiple headline stories reporting that Argentina's President Cristina Kirchner had adopted a Jewish boy in order to prevent him from becoming a werewolf, vampire or paranormal creature of that ilk.

And no, I am not making this up; it wasn't posted on the satirical **Onion**; you can fact check this for yourself. And, I hope that you will take the time and trouble to do that because this is good practice for those of us who still care about truth. Here in the U.S. this blatantly misleading, hyped-up nonsense, was featured in the Huffington Post, and in the UK Independent; picked up by Haaretz, Buzzfeed and then went viral as echo-chamber outlets around the world ran with this bizarre fable. Any number of pundits and online bloggers were quick to make use of this opportunity to poke fun at Mrs. Kirchner, Argentine politics and the Latin continent's rich tradition of magical-realism.

Few of these popular outlets bothered to post an update or make any effort to set the record straight since the real story is much less sensational. First of all, Mrs. Kirchner did not and has not adopted anyone and there are no Jewish vampires or werewolves either. As Argentine journalist Uki Goni (**The Real Odessa**) explained: by tradition, the 7th consecutive son or 7th consecutive daughter born to an Argentine family is eligible to become the godchild of the president. Not all qualify, since the honor is restricted to families with children born without babies of the opposite gender arriving anywhere in between. Until this month, this honor has only been bestowed on Christian babies; which also includes a gold medal and a fully paid educational scholarship.

Yair Tawail's parents, Shlomo and Nehama, applied for this Argentine state benefit when he was born in 1993 and they were denied on the basis of their religion. When these rules were changed in 2009 to include Jews, this 7th son a rabbi, now 21, was finally accepted. In her role as the current Argentine President, Cristina Kirchner made a well-publicized visit to their home in time to help the family light their Hanukah candles. Earlier this year she set another precedent by accepting the child of a Lesbian couple as a presidential godchild.

According to historian Daniel Balmaceda, this presidential custom began in Argentina in 1907 when Volga German immigrants from south-eastern Russia asked then President Jose Figueroa Alcorta to become godfather to their son. This couple wanted to maintain a custom from Tsarist Russia, where the Tsar was said to become godfather to the seventh of consecutive sons; and the New World Argentine president accepted this Old World responsibility.

This practice soon became law, and as Argentina's first woman president, Isabel Peron, widow of strongman, General Juan Peron, extended these benefits to 7th consecutive daughters, as well. While there was a time in Catholic Argentina when large families were common, present day couples usually bear only two or three offspring; significantly reducing the threat of werewolves being born into the local population.

So how did this tabloid-press version of werewolves and Jewish vampires get tangled up with this story of a long standing, changing with the times, apparently harmless, Argentine tradition?

In case you are wondering, being a Celt, I am not averse to the paranormal but I do not believe in vampires or werewolves. Nevertheless, I did so enjoy that movie, with Frank Langella hanging out at

"Dracula's Castle" carefully planning his shape-shifting agenda with the beautiful young ladies residing at the nearby, fog enshrouded manor house. This version of the immortal demon lover was filmed in Cornwall out on St. Michael's Mount, not all that far from my family's ancestral home in St. Just. And still, I recognize the need to remain mindful, while history has made clear that fiction and folklore often intersect and blur, over and over again; and we can expect no end to this ongoing process, which may be exploited during any number of current and future political agendas.

So, it seems that something like a conflation-dynamic has probably transpired in this recent mass misperception of events in Argentina; carried world-wide with the irresponsible, sensation-seeking media. As always, there is a back-story available for those willing to dig at least somewhat deeper into this over–amped, global, media travesty. Apparently, there was a time when East European superstitions included a belief that seventh consecutive sons were cursed to become werewolves or vampires and a similar belief held that 7th consecutive daughters were doomed to become witches. These doomed sons were expected to transform into werewolves on the first Friday after their 13th birthday. Reportedly, this superstition was strong enough to result in many seventh-born being rejected, adopted out, abandoned or even killed at birth. As a result, frightened parents sought the protection of the Tsar.

Somehow or other, by a process best left to cultural historians, these old East European superstitions were conflated with totally unrelated, Guarani indigenous folklore which persists out and around the Argentine cattle-raising Pampas. Should you wander out into these far-flung territories in Patagonia, local gauchos may spin some tall-tales of their *lobizon*, a human which transforms into a pig or dog every Tuesday or Friday night, not just once a month under a full Moon. Unlike other werewolf legends, the *lobizon* does not transmit its curse through a bite but rather by passing through the legs of its unfortunate victims. Enough said and you have been duly warned!

President Cristina Fernadez Kirchner has now become godmother to some 700 children since taking office in 2007. And, it does seem that presidential protection may be working after all, since there have been no authenticated reports of Jewish or any other ethnically-specific werewolves or vampires anywhere throughout Argentine history, although I am not so sure about witches.

FEBRUARY

Twelve Minutes in Sedona

"Actors are agents of change. A film, a piece of theater... can make a difference. It can change the world". (Alan Rickman, Actor)

"In times of universal deceit, telling the truth is a revolutionary act". (George Orwell)

"The great enemy of truth is very often not the lie, deliberate, contrived and dishonest, but the myth, persuasive and unrealistic". (John F. Kennedy)

We have an early spring here in Northern Arizona and are celebrating our 21st Sedona International Film Festival. This year's event is being held in observation of the 100th anniversary of the birthday of renowned actor, director and former Sedona resident Orson Welles. Academy and Golden Globe Award winner Richard Dreyfuss is in town to receive a Lifetime Achievement Award and also recognition for his role as activist and spokesperson on the issue of media informing policy, legislation, public opinion; and in expression of his sentiments in favor of privacy, freedom of speech, democracy and individual accountability. (SedonaFilmFestival.Org).

Acting legend, Ed Asner is also here for an opening-night screening of his latest film, **Good Men.** Now 85, Asner has served two terms as President of the Screen Actor's Guild, won seven Emmy Awards and served as an outspoken advocate of universal health care and worker's rights. In his role in **Good Men,** the veteran actor and activist has taken on a personal issue which he says remains untouchable in Hollywood and therefore appropriate for the spirit of independence in the independent film industry. The result is a film only 12 minutes in length, written and directed by Brian Connors and produced with a mini-budget by Sean Tracy.

Essentially a one act comedy with only two actors, Ed and Mark Rydell portray two elderly long-time friends and colleagues who argue about the conspiracy allegations surrounding the events of September 11, 2001. This emotionally charged character study was shot in one day with two 5D cameras. Asner's character argues for the massive evidence that the World Trade Center's Twin Towers and Building 7 were brought down by explosive demolitions, as is believed to be the case by 2,000

Architects and Engineers for 9/11 Truth, founded in 2006, who call officialdom's original investigations and ongoing stories, a sham. (ae911truth.org).

Moreover, Pilots for 9/11 Truth, also founded in 2006 by aviation professionals, have presented deeply serious, thoroughly-researched challenges to all official investigations. (PilotsFor9/11Truth.org). Asner's friend, portrayed by Mark Rydell angrily rejects any and all unofficial explanations as unpatriotic "conspiracies". Now, nearly 15 years after 9/11, these 12 minutes of film brilliantly capture an ongoing and heated debate throughout this dangerously polarized country, as to "what really happened ".

On the theme of "conspiracy" allegations I find it interesting to note that the term "conspiracy theory" was coined by the CIA in April 1967. Their Clandestine Services unit then focused on strategies for discrediting any and all unwelcome inquiries, including the use of the word conspiracy in a pejorative sense in order to debunk and discredit. (washingtonsblog.com, February 23, 2015). In recent times, we have an Orwellian twist given to the word "truth" so that those who doubt official propaganda and mass-media lies, are ridiculed and dismissed as conspiracy-theory "truthers". (see also: David Martin, "Thirteen Techniques for Truth Suppression", brasscheck.com).

In a number of interviews surrounding the release of *Good Men,* Asner has been repeatedly asked why he thought that Hollywood would never produce such a film. In general, he often replied that the current mood in Tinsel-Town is one of "go along to get along", a reluctance to speak truth to power, challenge authority or the fairy tale myth of a free and democratic Republic of America. On a darker note, Asner observes that most of the group-think, bobble-headed populace can't handle the idea that America would allow anything like the 9/11 attacks to be done to itself.

While the veteran actor denies the existence of an official Hollywood Blacklist, he affirms the reality that political views and activities can also severely impact one's professional life. Asner admits to feeling such pressures, and his immensely popular TV series, **Lou Grant** was abruptly canceled in 1982 due to right wing protest campaigns against his criticism of U.S. foreign policy in Central America. With an eye toward history, Hollywood and the entertainment industry has a long and colorful tradition of political censorship.

This overt form of scare-mongering oppression, peaked during the mid-twentieth century with the Blacklist policy of denying employment to actors, directors, screenwriters, musicians and other entertainers, due to suspected political beliefs and associations. During the years when Ronald Reagan was president of the Screen Actors Guild, he kept in close touch with "better dead than red", FBI Director, J. Edgar Hoover; who conducted notorious and highly publicized "witch hunts" against allegedly disloyal public personalities. Less than 10 % of those investigated by the House Un-American Activities Committee (HUAC) were able to return to their careers as a result of this anti-communist hysteria. (Dan Georgakas, "The Hollywood Blacklist", english.illinois.edu, 1992).

Now, following the world changing events of September 11, 2001, censorship in the entertainment industry remains; although at a much subtler level than we saw during the dark days of the Hollywood Blacklist. For now, at least, alternative media outlets and the international, independent film industry are still able to offer creative options outside of the establishment control-matrix.

MARCH

Grey Wolf

"If you tell a lie big enough and keep repeating it, people will eventually come to believe it. The lie can maintained only for such a time as the State can shield the people from the political, economic and/or military consequences of the lie. It thus becomes vitally important for the State to use all of its powers to repress dissent, for truth is the mortal enemy of the lie, and thus by extension, truth is the greatest enemy of the State". (Joseph Goebbels, Reich Minister of Propaganda, 1897-1945)

"In wartime, truth is so precious that she should always be attended by a bodyguard of lies". (Winston Churchill,1943)

"If you win, you need not have to explain… If you lose, you should not be there to explain". (Adolf Hitler, 1889-?)

'"History is a version of the past that people have decided to agree upon". (Napoleon Bonaparte)

"Who controls the past controls the future. Who controls the present controls the past". (George Orwell, 1903-1950)

Until recently I had relegated those reports of Hitler in Argentina to the same category as tabloid sightings of Elvis. However, newly de-classified FBI documents reveal that our government knew that Adolf Hitler was alive and living in Argentina long after the end of World

War II. (Lisa Pattrick, http://topinfopost.com, February, 12, 2014).

Moreover, neither Stalin, Churchill, Truman, Franco or then General, Eisenhower believed that suicide in the bunker story; propagated by Medieval-historian Hugh Trevor-Roper (1914-2003).

Consider, if you will, the disturbing fact that this young medievalist was assigned by British intelligence to write an account of the Führer's final days in his Berlin bunker; despite the fact that he had absolutely no academic background in Teutonic history or politics, and could neither read nor speak German. As a result, his account of that supposed double-suicide of Hitler and Eva Braun was based upon the testimony of surviving "witnesses"; all über- loyal Nazis, who were more than willing to say whatever this naïve young historian wanted to hear. (**The Last Days of Hitler**,1947). In fact, there exists no forensic evidence whatsoever that Hitler and Eva died in the bunker, as was dramatized in the 2004 movie **Downfall**, starring Bruno Ganz as the creepily charismatic Führer.

Apparently, Trevor-Roper's MI-6 sponsored suicide

story was an important propaganda basis for Allied efforts to rebuild a new Germany without any hopes that their Führer could return... and also to promote a belief that if Hitler was dead, then Nazism was also dead. The notoriously arrogant Trevor-Roper's credibility was seriously and deservedly damaged in 1983 when he "authenticated" those **Hitler Diaries** subsequently proven to be forgeries. (Richard J. Evans, **Lying About Hitler**, 2002).

Recent publication of **Grey Wolf: The Escape of Adolf Hitler** (2011) by Simon Dunstan and Gerard Williams, now serves to shed some much-needed light into the shadowy endgame strategies that existed toward the close of World War II. Their title is especially apt, given that from early on, Adolf Hitler used the *nom de guerre* Grey Wolf. In Old High German the name Adolf translates into "noble wolf". It was as Herr Wolf that he was introduced to 17 year old, high-spirited, shallow-minded, shop girl, Eva Braun; and to many intimate acquaintances he was addressed as Uncle Wolf. His younger sister Paula changed her surname to Wolf in an attempt to retain some degree of privacy. Hitler's yacht was called the Sea Wolf, his plane Flying Wolf, his field headquarters in East Prussia were known as the Wolf's Lair, in Ukraine it was Werewolf and in France, Wolf's Gorge. His fearsome U-boats were known as wolf-packs and grey wolves and one of them, code named Gruppe Seewolf, reportedly delivered Hitler to Argentina where he spent his declining years as the proverbial Grey Wolf. (p. xxxi).

While it is true that party loyalists died in and around the Führerbunker's multi-leveled, subterranean, bomb-shelter complex beneath the Reichs Chancellery in Berlin; Hitler and Eva Braun were likely not among them. According to multiple accounts, the two escaped, in agreement with plans set in motion by Hitler's ever-present, "Brown Eminence", Reichsleiter, and Head of the Party Chancellery, Martin Bormann. It is both well known and not unusual for world leaders to employ body doubles; Stalin had numerous stand-ins and Churchill at least one. Hitler had six of these lookalikes. His favorite, Gustav Weber, had been standing-in for the Führer since July 20, 1944 when the bomb attempt at Wolf's Lair Field Headquarters, left Hitler with recurrent after-effects from shock and injuries. More specifically, an increasingly suspicious Hitler was also plagued by infected facial and painful nasal cavity wounds inflicted by airborne wood splinters from an oak table that had shielded him from the full force of the blast.

While alive, Weber's final impersonation of Hitler took place during the last officially photographed newsreel appearance when Weber handed out medals to a row of Hitler Youth recipients on March 20th, 1945. Herr Weber could be distinguished from Hitler's other doubles by a palsied tremor of his left hand, which led to speculation that the Führer himself suffered from Parkinson's disease. Weber's final service to his master was carried out in a double suicide scenario orchestrated by Bormann.

Eva Braun's double was selected from a cadre of willing young actresses that propaganda minister Joseph Goebbels had maintained for his own amusement, along with another canine double for Hitler's beloved Alsatian Shepherd Blondi. This counterfeit Führer and his bogus bride were taken into private quarters to enact their final scenario. Weber was shot and the gullible actress and unfortunate dog poisoned with cyanide, on April 30, 1945; also the date of a German pagan holiday, Walpurgis Night, made famous in the Bram Stoker novel **Dracula.**

Meanwhile, another plan was already in motion. Hitler, Eva, Blondi, Bormann, former Gestapo Chief Heinrich Mueller and a small group of others, allegedly slipped out of their bunker in order to board a waiting plane reportedly flown by SS Captain and Luftwaffe pilot Peter Eric Baumgart. ("Luftwaffe pilot sent to jail for five years", Warsaw, August 8, 1949, **Canberra Times,** August 9, 1949). On May 2, 1945 German radio announced: "The Führer is dead. Long live the Reich!" Shortly thereafter, Soviet troops officially entered the underground complex. However, it is now known that some few days earlier, a special detachment of SMERSH (NKVD) counter espionage element, especially created by Stalin, had already entered this enclave in order to discover the whereabouts of Hitler, dead or alive. Absolutely no evidence of the deaths of either Hitler or Eva Braun were ever found.

Next to arrive were 12 women doctors from the Red Army medical corp. Their leader, who spoke fluent

German, immediately demanded of the remaining occupants: "Where is Hitler and where are the "glad rags"? After a thorough search, these determined Russian women, on a dedicated mission, found neither Hitler's body, nor a shred of Eva's furs or any of her party-girl wardrobe. The following day, the Soviet official periodical **Pravda,** declared, "The announcement of Hitler's death was a fascist trick". (James P. O'Donnell, **The Bunker, 1**978).

Details of the historic escape from Berlin and the flight routes thereafter differ. In Harry Cooper's account, (**Hitler in Argentina**, 2014) Bormann drugged the unwilling suicidal couple in order to save them and flew them to Oslo where Eva died of the drug overdose. With the reported source of this version being Bormann himself, I could imagine some strategic disinformation agenda designed to discourage anyone from looking for her and their children, after she left the marriage in 1954. More about that speculation, later. Additional information on Cooper's ongoing investigations can be found at: http://sharkhunters.com, along with alleged plans for the "relocation of the Reich".

Given a likely motivation for dis-information, the flight plan set forth in **Grey Wolf** seems to make more sense. According to this well documented version, escapees from the war zone were flown to a clandestine facility in Denmark and then from there on to Spain. Aided by General Franco's pro-fascist regime, they were then flown on to another secret base in the Spanish Canary Islands, located off the coast of West Africa. After a much needed rest, the group undertook a lengthy, dangerous undersea journey, via a Grey Wolf U-boat, to the coast of Argentina and then, after another rest, transported to their new home in Patagonia.

This choice of refuge and safe-haven seems logical since Patagonia and San Carlos de Bariloche in particular, has been a de-facto German overseas colony since the late nineteenth century. I have been a grateful guest there and have enjoyed their spectacular lake and alpine landscape setting with Bavarian architecture strongly reminiscent of southern Germany, as well as authentic beer and bratwurst amply supplied by local German-speaking town folk. As my local hosts explained, during and after World War II, pro-fascist dictator Juan Peron, an ardent admirer of Mussolini,

Hitler and Franco, had enthusiastically welcomed a strong Nazi presence in Argentina and hosted the largest Nazi party outside of Germany. Peron even sent a "Blue Division" to assist Hitler during the German war on the Russian front. (Uki Goni, **The Real Odessa: How Peron Brought The Nazi War Criminals to Argentina,** 2002).

During my visit to Bariloche I learned that refugee Germans, "war criminals" or not, were accorded something akin to "rock-star" celebrity status. Local friends and colleagues were kind enough to provide me with a copy of Argentine journalist Abel Basti's, **Hitler Died in Argentina** (1987). While Basti admitted that he fabricated some of his material in order to avoid trouble with Argentine authorities, (probably wise) he nevertheless maintains that the salient facts are true. And so, my patient friends and colleagues agreed to take me along his suggested tour of Nazi-related sights; including plastic-surgery clinics disguised as holiday chalets. Later in the day, we undertook a steep uphill hike to a stone and cement-block watch tower/bunker constructed upon a cliff overseeing a sheltered cove, where clandestine submarines could discharge their high value passengers under cover of darkness.

For those unfamiliar with South American geography, this region is very close to the Chilean border. Therefore, if a hasty escape should become necessary, one can readily arrange transport by ship or over any one of several routes across the Andean Cordillera. Local word has it that many of these intrepid fugitives actually made their way on foot and some say skis, all the way over and across the formidable Andean cordillera toward safe-haven within Chile.

For well over a decade, I have been offering systemically oriented social trauma seminars and trainings in Latin America. My professional home, now in Mexico City, was formerly located in Argentina. During that time, much of my work was generously sponsored by my Spanish language publisher Alma Lepik, in Buenos Aires. In Bariloche, Neuquén, Rosario and Buenos Aires, my trans-generational trauma seminars inevitably engaged many children, grandchildren and other descendants, relatives and loved ones of refugees who arrived during and after the fall of the Third Reich; as well as a number of their surviving victims.

A perpetrator/victim dynamic, with all of its complexities, comprises an integral part of trans-generational trauma work and this was especially evident while working with this aspect of modern Latin American history. In brief, to me at least, it seems quite evident that descendants of perpetrators and victims suffer, both equally and also differently. While I am tempted to write more about this phenomenon and the often mysterious bond between perpetrators and their victims, Bert Hellinger has already done so; and his timely and often provocative observations in articles, books and video materials, have been translated into many languages .

Soon after World War II came to a close, thousands of fascist refugees, collaborators and their families, found their way down to South America via a "monastery route" along Vatican organized and protected "ratlines"; overseen by Bishop Alois Hudol, Monsignor Krunoslav Draganovi, (who worked for the CIA), and hundreds of other Catholic clergy. (Peter Levenda, **Ratline: Soviet Spies, Nazi Priests and the Disappearance of Adolf Hitler,** 2012). False passports and new identities were issued along with permission to board passenger and freighter ships headed south.

Soon these ratlines, as they were named by allied intelligence, extended across and throughout the southern continent. In time notorious war criminals such as (CIA agent), Klaus Barbie, "Butcher of Lyon" and Walter Rauff, (inventor of portable gas chambers), felt safe enough to openly serve as "security advisers" to Latin American dictators, determined to crush dissent. An abundance of well-researched documentation of these Nazi contributions to fascism throughout South America is available in the above mentioned Argentine journalist, Uki Goni's, **The Real Odessa** (2002).

Nazi refugees found a welcome home in Chile where they established a heavily armed German speaking colony which soon became a state within a state, (rumored to have ties to the CIA, as well). This Nazi enclave located high in the Andes, south of Santiago de Chile in the Maule region, also served as a safe house for war criminals on the run. After our

Nixon/Kissinger regime supported a CIA engineered September 11,1973 coup, ousting democratically elected, leftist President Salvador Allende, and installing General Augusto Pinochet, the Colonia Dignidad (Villa Baviera) became a torture and interrogation center for this extreme right wing regime. Here it is important to be clear that not only German and Chilean fascists were involved in torture. The horrific torture chamber at Colonia Dignidad was designed by American CIA operative and professional assassin Michael Townley, now living somewhere under our Federal Witness Protection Program. (John Dignes, **The Condor Years: How Pinochet And His Allies Brought Terrorism To Three Continents,** 2005).

Under Pinochet, Operation Condor's "war on terror ", waged against leftists and other suspected "dissidents", was officially launched in 1975 and eventually spread throughout many other South American countries; installing fascist military dictatorships, and spies, informers, kidnappers, and secret police, who sadistically tortured, incarcerated and "disappeared" at least 60,000 people of all ages. This period, now known as the "Dirty Wars", continued to carry out these atrocities until 1985. Dirty War fascists were actively aided and supported by our US foreign policy, up to and through the Ronald Reagan years, based upon a paranoid fear of a communist takeover down there, "right in our own back yard". (Saul Landau, "Terrorism Then and Now", **Counterpunch,** August 20-21, 2005).

Under Bormann's masterful direction, and with powerful Vatican support, the Nazi network had apparently successfully metastasized; taken deep root in South America, and was wielding a powerful fascist influence throughout the continent. As a result, the quasi-mystical personality cult surrounding the Führer was no longer so important. Hitler himself had apparently settled into a quieter life and enjoyed time recovering from his various ailments at the Hotel Eden Spa in La Falda, owned by Nazi sympathizers Walter and Ida Eichhorn.

Service personnel from the now abandoned resort, recall visits of very special guests about which they were told to say nothing whatsoever, ever. Housekeeper Catelina Gomero recalls these mysterious guests as polite and reclusive during their visits. Another worker, Hernan Ancin observed a polite, rather gaunt, Hitler and his "well fed " wife during 5 visits between 1953 and 1954. He specifically remembered Eva as someone, world-weary, who appeared to have suffered a great deal. Apparently, she had grown increasingly heavy and unable to shed any weight after the birth of her last child. Both hotel workers, already elderly at the time of their interviews, received death threats and declined further access. (Jorge Camarasa, "*La Falda tiene tambien su secreto nazi*" **La Nacion**, Buenos Aires, July 27,1980).

There is not much in the way of reliable information regarding Hitler's children. According to the wife of his former Secretary of State Otto Meissner, a son, Helmut, was born to Magda Goebbels in 1935, the result of a passionate affair with her Führer while both were vacationing at the Baltic sea in 1934. Magda subsequently poisoned their nine year old boy, together with her five daughters, shortly before committing suicide with her husband just outside of the Führerbunker.

Hitler also reportedly had a daughter Gisela with athlete Othilie (Gold Tilly) Fleischer; "a true representative of the Aryan race", Nazi Olympian and gold medal winner from the 1936 Berlin games. It seems that he only saw the child once. (Gisela Heuser, **Adolf Hitler, Mon Pere,** 1966). Her mother denies the story.

There are also reports that Eva Braun's first child, Ursula, "Uschi" was born in San Remo, Italy on December 31, 1938, and this birth was confirmed by her father. The child was later raised at Berchtesgaden as a child of Eva's friend Gitta Schneider, and was extensively photographed there along with affectionate family album pictures of Hitler and Eva with this small blond girl ("Americans Find Treasure Chest of Eva Braun", **St. Petersburg Times**, November 16, 1945). After the war, Ursula was said to be the daughter of Eva's sister Gretel Braun and her husband Hermann Fegelein, yet their only child, Eva, was born after the war ended. When six year old Uschi arrived in Argentina in 1945, her mother was again pregnant with a second daughter, although this was her third pregnancy. Eva Braun's mother Franziska Braun, when interviewed by the Allies, said that there was a second stillborn child in 1943. (North American Newspaper Alliance, February 18, 1946).

While Hitler and his guardians felt fairly secure during the time when Peron was in power, when that was no longer the case, Hitler and his family were reportedly moved to a more remote and therefore more secure location. Eva apparently found it difficult to adapt to such a dull and rural existence. There were no more parties, and her often morose husband, 23 years her senior, without a cadre of inner circle admirers, was probably not the best of company. Eventually, in 1954, Eva Braun-Hitler and their two daughters are said to have fled to Neuquen province where they were continuously looked after by party loyalists.

As the aging Führer's health issues increased in his final years, together with the last in a succession of Blondis; his personal physician, Dr. Otto Lehmann (may not be his real name) and long-time valet Heinrich Bethe, kept him as comfortable as possible despite torments of dementia, delusions, hallucinations and nightmares, involving vengeful ghosts of his murdered millions. According to this version of history, Adolf Hitler died on February 13, 1962. In the interest of secrecy, his remaining caretakers then became a liability to the Organization. Bethe knew this and managed an escape to Chile. He changed his name to Juan Paulovsky and succeeded in living out his days in the small coastal town of Caleta Olivia. Dr. Lehmann was not so lucky and disappeared shortly afterward, probably murdered. **(Grey Wolf)**.

So now, what to believe? Certainly not MI-6 agent for hire, Trevor-Roper. An important question here might be "Just exactly who benefits from that bunker suicide story or those rumors of Hitler as an asexual, impotent, pervert?

What we do know, at this point, is that Monastery Routes and Vatican-operated ratlines were absolutely real, Peron was a dedicated fascist, and many Nazi war criminals have been extradited from South America. The USA/CIA supported "Dirty Wars" were absolutely real, all those disappeared really were tortured and killed and Colonia Dignidad was, and is real, as well. Now, many critics of Hitler in Argentina accounts, have maintained that Martin Bormann could not have possibly escaped from Berlin and orchestrated and secured a vast Nazi network in South America. Never mind that there are too many accounts of his Brown Eminence in Latin America to be readily dismissed.

Recent, so called, forensic evidence, has surfaced claiming that Martin Bormann's skull has been retrieved from a dig in Berlin in 1972 and its DNA analyzed in 1998 perfectly matches with an elderly relative, who remains unnamed. Never mind that this site had been previously excavated with no bones found, whatsoever. From my perspective, even more interesting is the fact that the Bormann skull contained traces of a sticky red clay not found anywhere near the section of Berlin where it was supposedly found. In fact, this volcanic red clay is ubiquitous in Paraguay - a type common to the village of Ita. This does suggest that Bormann died elsewhere and then his skull was deliberately planted in order to be "found ".

Who, we might now ask, would be most likely to benefit from such an elaborate deception? Esteemed forensic surgeon W.H. Thomas also examined this skull, and clearly indicated that some dental-work had been carried out long after 1945. (W.H. Thomas, independent.co.uk, August, 11 1996). A supposition such as this then opens a way to the salient question - exactly why, and exactly who, would be sufficiently motivated to go to such lengths for such an elaborate deception; unless there was great deal of very sensitive information to conceal.

One could speculate that Bormann's survival could prove embarrassing to the Allies who sentenced him to death, in abstentia, during their Nuremberg show trials, as well as to those Israelis who either failed or were unwilling to capture him; or to our own CIA who would prefer that any contact with him and his infernal machinations never happened. For an in-depth exploration of Bormann, both the man and the myth, see the late Paul Manning's courageous, **Martin Bormann: Nazi in Exile, (**1981); while bearing in mind that soon after its publication his publisher's legs were broken and Manning's son murdered. The author died shortly thereafter.

From my perspective, it seems that many of these

accounts of high level Nazi deaths and disappearances need to be viewed with considerable caution. Historians and journalists know that it is the very nature of governments to lie, especially in matters they deem sensitive for "national security". How many of those supposedly "disappeared" or "suicide", dead Nazi's actually turned up among the thousands who arrived here in the USA along with Werner von Braun under "Operation Paperclip"? This was, of course, deemed necessary for our "national security", during our post-war space and nuclear weapons race with the Soviets, immediately following World War II. War criminals or not, these Nazi scientists arrived safely in the supposedly democratic republic of the United States of America, via our own version of the ratline covert operations. This was a post-war real-politic of "never mind their fascist ideologies, we need their rocket science ".

During this era of trading principles for power, we might consider, for example, the case of Hans Kammler, who supposedly "disappeared" right after the war. Kammler was an undesirable ally by any reasonable standard, given that he oversaw construction of underground slave labor facilities and concentration camps and engineered other creative means of mass-extermination. More important, it seems, is that Kammler also had intimate knowledge and expertise from the Nazi V2 rocket project, as well as involvement in a secret aerospace weapon known as *Die Glocke* (The Bell). In his book: **The Hunt for Zero Point: Inside the Classified World of Antigravity Technology** (2001), Nick Cook raised the possibility that Kammler came over to America with his Paperclip colleagues. In **Reich of the Black Sun** (2005), Joseph P. Farrell tends to agree that this is a real possibility; and aerospace engineer Clark McClelland who worked at NASA from 1958-1992, in his online "Stargate Chronicles", specifically stated that Kammler was there at NASA along with a prototype for The Bell.

More information about Paperclip Nazis is available in Annie Jacobsen's: **Operation Paperclip: The Secret Intelligence That Brought Nazi Scientists To America,** (2015) and Eric Lichtblau's, **The Nazis Next Door: How America Became a Safe Haven for Hitler's Men,** (2014), which details how the CIA, FBI and our military, put Hitler's minions to work as spies, and intelligence assets while white-washing their criminal pasts.

So now, here in 2015, we can rest assured that the man, Adolf Hitler born in 1889, really and truly is finally, absolutely dead and Bormann, as well. The time, dates and circumstances of their demise may never be established to the satisfaction of all concerned. While those dashing, Hugo Boss designed uniforms for the SS and Wehrmacht are now seen only in the movies, Nazism is alive and well and thriving under many and various rubrics. On the subject of controversies surrounding the post-war survival of The Führer, Peter Levenda offers the following: Look around. Neo-Nazism is on the rise. There is a hard swing to the right in many countries around the world, some of it provoked by fears of a terrorist threat. The instability of the global economies and widening gap between rich and poor is a familiar precedent for the appearance of populist dictators. Civil liberties are being eroded in the name of national security. Military and political leaders are warming their hands on today's version of the Reichstag fire. In Latin America, and Asia, Hitler is more popular than ever.

What the Allies feared would happen, did happen. As the story of Hitler's suicide is shown to be unsupportable by the evidence, a resurgence of belief in this monomaniacal madman and his fanatical ideology of race, purity, and power is guaranteed. Like Barbarossa he sleeps in a cave, perhaps in a salt mine in Salzburg, or more comfortably in a guest house in Bolzano, in some "monastery in Tibet " or a tropical isle in Southeast Asia –   in wait for the hurt, hate-filled and willingly ignorant to call his name in their hour of need. (**Ratlines**).

Stolpersteine

"While some of us debate what history is or was, others take it into their own hands". (Michel Rolp Trouillot)

"Mourning has validity at both the individual and collective level, in the intra-psychic and the interactive. It involves pain, work and discovery ". (P.C. Racamier, **La genie des origins)**

Following the Nazi organized genocide during the 1940s, many of the survivors emerged with a compelling need to bear witness and a compelling conviction of the importance of doing so, in part, as an atonement for their survival. They were largely ignored until much later when what became known as the Holocaust, became a topic of interest aided by advent of the 1961 Adolf Eichmann trial in Jerusalem. While the events of this genocidal era have often been referred to as "unimaginable" or "unspeakable", these epithets have also served as reasons for neither imagining nor speaking about such a horrific episode, and so we are excused from further inquiry.

If memorials to commemorate wars are difficult, commemoration of a genocide is even more so … and the political stakes are equally high. Unlike war memorials devoted to those who sacrificed themselves for some greater cause, this notion of meaningful sacrifice does not pertain to those former citizens whom the state has turned against as "enemies within". (Jenny Elkins, **Trauma and the Memory of Politics,** 2003).

In a recent issue of **The New Yorker**, journalist Elizabeth Kolbert, who's own great-grandmother was "disappeared" during the Nazi Holocaust, explores the phenomenon of the Stolpersteine; a public art-project and the work of German conceptual artist and sculptor, Gunter Demnig. Born in 1947 in Berlin, Demnig now resides in Cologne. In stark contrast to most memorials designed to command attention, his understated Stolpersteine, (stumbling blocks) reside quite literally underfoot. Each piece consists of a block of concrete onto which a brass plaque has been carefully affixed.

These blocks, which are 10x10 cm, approximately the size of a Rubik's Cube, or a child's hand, are embedded into a walkway, or lowered in among cobblestones, in a manner which results in the surface of these plaques lying nearly flush with the pavement. Each plaque is stamped by hand, as a gesture, according to Demnig, deliberately expressed in opposition to the mechanized, bureaucratic mass murder, executed within the extensive slave-labor and extermination camps operating with impunity during the entire Third Reich (1933-1945). (**A Stone for My Great-Grandmother**, newyorker.com, 2/16, 2015).

Stolperststeine, a term which roughly translates as something close to "Stumbling Stones", are carefully hand -crafted in order to commemorate all Jews, Roma, Sinti, dissidents, blacks, homosexuals, Jehovah's Witnesses, Freemasons, military deserters, resistance fighters and communists, who were deported and exterminated. These small metal plaques also commemorate the mentally and physically disabled victims of euthanasia, as well as those who survived incarceration and sterilization clinics, or were forced to immigrate or committed suicide as a result of Nazi persecution. Each stone has one name, date of birth, date taken away and date and manner of death, if known; then they are placed into the ground outside of this individual's last known address or workplace. The time and date of each installation is announced in local news outlets for the benefit of those who would like to attend. At this point, Demnig says that increasing numbers of such victims are much too great and now his project needs to be understood as largely symbolic; and yet, he continues.

Whenever possible, the artist endeavors to lay these stones himself, in the presence of those who commissioned each piece, as he travels around in a minivan with an assistant and their essential tools. In silence, Demnig kneels down, with one knee covered with a protective leather pad, clears out a designated space, inserts the stones, adjusts them into place, and finally adds cement and water. He then steps back to survey his work, brushes off plaques and cleans them with a cloth. Demnig remembers one installation where people from four countries gathered to attend, without previous knowledge of one another, and soon discovered that they were all related.

Anyone can sponsor a plaque's manufacture and installation for family, friends, neighbors or co-workers, by contacting info@stolpersteine.eu. Demnig began implanting his Stolpersteine in 1995. His first cubic pieces were placed on public land, at the request of survivors, in Cologne without permission, and a second group installed in Berlin, also without permission. Both cities eventually legalized these emotionally laden, heavy, "stones".

As the number of those who had actually witnessed the Holocaust diminished, interest in Stolpersteine actually grew, in almost reverse proportion. In Berlin, residents gathered in order to discover the identities of those who had been deported right out from their own neighborhoods. Information came from rumors, schools, relatives, and various organizations such as Yad Vashem in Jerusalem. As the project grew, students in various cities and countries volunteered to raise funds and help.

As this endeavor eventually spread to other German cities, it also took root in other countries; including Holland, Belgium, Italy, France, Luxembourg, Austria, Russia, Hungary, Croatia, Norway, Poland, Ukraine, Slovenia, Slovakia and the Czech Republic. At present there are more than six thousand Stolpersteine in Berlin, together with more than 50,000 others embedded within public grounds throughout Europe. The Stolpersteine project has now been identified as the "largest decentralized, grass roots memorial in the world".

Demnig's choice of stumbling stones as an artistic vehicle for his memorial project is particularly apt, given an old folk story in pre-Holocaust Germany, that it was a custom for non-Jews to say, whenever they stumbled over a stone, "there must be a Jew buried here". (Jüde als Schimpfwort Archiv, Raid-rus, 28 March, 2007). These stumbling blocks, as metaphor made manifest, and the slight uneasiness that they create along pedestrian walkways, serve to unbalance routine steps and interrupt the smooth progress of many would-be, upright and upstanding citizens. Some of these small scale, brass stumbling blocks may even cause some pain. Nevertheless, their humble, earth-bound, solid, cuboid presence carries an existential invitation.

Stolpersteine, now buried within many a common ground, lie there and wait; as a timeless expression of hope. Their very presence, in those places where they have been accepted, suggests that at least some of our awake and aware and otherwise willing, kind souls, might pause for a moment, to bend a knee toward the ground, in order to read what is written on each plaque, about the crimes involving both victims and perpetrators. Upon each installation the Stolpersteine shine bright with metallic luster and in time this brass will tarnish. Those living nearby are often asked to keep them polished as a gesture of renewal and to stave off indifference and oblivion. (Ruth Breuer, ARAS Connections, # 3, 2012).

Not everyone has been or is currently receptive to installations of Stolpersteine and this memorial project has been met with a number of past and ongoing stumbling blocks along their way. In Munich, for example, the city's Jewish community rejected these plaques as undignified, on grounds that they did not represent an appropriate venue for remembering the Shoah. More specifically, many felt that they would simply offer another opportunity for German jack boots and other "good Germans" to symbolically demean and trample over their Jewish victims. In response, Demnig rejected their suggestion that these brass plaques should be placed on walls, since he feels that people tend to ignore plaques on buildings, whereas they consistently look down to the ground. (http://moreintelligentlife.com, May/June, 2013).

In addition and not unexpectedly, Neo-Nazis and their sympathizers have vandalized Stolpersteine in many countries, by painting them over, as well as removing them entirely, in order for these memorial stones to be ritually and otherwise, destroyed. There are more than a few "Holocaust deniers" who steadfastly maintain that the administrative killing of millions never actually happened. The Nazis' genocidal enterprise sought to cover up their tracks and they nearly succeeded. A survivor remembers the diabolical warning to the inhabitants of their camp:

However this war may end, we have won the war against you; none of you will be left to bear witness, but even if someone were to survive, the world would not believe him. There will perhaps be suspicions, discussions, research by historians, but there will be no certainties, because we will destroy the evidence together with you. And even if some proof should remain, and some of you survive, people will say that the events you describe are too monstrous to be believed, they will say that they are exaggerations of

Allied propaganda and will believe us, who will deny everything, and not you. We will be the ones to dictate the history of our Lagers. (Simon Weisenthal: **The Murderers Among Us,** 1967).

Disturbing as this may be for some, truth is that this ancient, deeply rooted, sadistically cruel and ongoing mindset, which briefly manifested as Nazism, has also survived the Holocaust. More or perhaps even equally important, is that an independent conceptual-artist, who cares rather more than any politician with a self-serving agenda, has found a culturally specific way to offer a grass-roots, cross-culturally adaptable option for honoring the "disappeared". Here we have a heartfelt humanistic challenge, not limited in time or space to Germany, or Nazi victims and perpetrators, since the tragedy of the disappeared is a long standing, ongoing world-wide phenomenon, not safely limited to the past. Demnig's Stolpersteine project makes clear that in the genuine interest of healing, the humanities and related arts may have even more to offer than politics and those closely related seductive illusions of some official justice.

APRIL

Treasure Map

"....behind every map's information is what's left out, the un-mapped and un-mappable". (Rebecca Solnit)

"There was a single blue line of crayon drawn across every wall in the house. 'What does it mean', I asked. 'A pirate needs the sight of the sea', he said." (Brian Andreas, **Story People)**

" When I was about five, I think, I desperately wanted to be a pirate and have the hat and all ". (Keira Knightly)

"The songs of our ancestors are also the songs of our children" . (Philip Carr-Gomm, Arch Druid of Sussex)

Over the years of presenting systemically oriented, family constellation work, participants often ask how this work could be of value when they have either no or very little information about their family system. In response I often offer a linear option of contacting organizations that exist in order to document and explore genealogical information; and many of their skilled librarians can be very helpful, even with minimal information. Another, non-linear option, well known to shamans and indigenous medicine-people, lies in a willingness to contact the Greater Informational Field, which is also interactive. The challenge then is, with an appropriate level of humility, to set an intention, formulate respectful questions, and remain open-minded and receptive and then wait.

In my experience, this timeless Field has many ways of communicating important and timely information; including dreams, coincidences, synchronicity, a freak accident, or perhaps a mysterious and persistent symptom. Information from this non-linear and timeless source often arrives in non-linear sequences. There are also times when we may have some information, but something of which are unaware may need to make itself known; and The Field can find ways to communicate this information, as well.

While I have been researching my family history for decades now, hidden information has been revealed in several interesting ways…sometimes like a treasure hunt…one clue at a time. One summer when my daughter was about eight she received an invitation to a birthday party designed as a pirate's treasure map. This pirate theme-party was going to be only for girls and guests were requested to attend in costume. While I thought that this was an unusual theme for a little girl's party, my daughter was enthusiastic and we set about putting together her costume...which soon developed into an unexpected obsession.

My then, 20th Century , American eight year old was quite suddenly very clear about exactly how her costume should come together; hat, boots, cummerbund-sash, together with just the right authentic looking plastic sword, and we may have found some sort of rubber dagger, just in case. And this process went on and on until I realized that something else was happening...past life maybe or perhaps some unknown systemic entanglement.

After she was safely asleep, I telephoned my Cornish mother who had always told us about our virtuous, hardworking, Cornish ancestors who had lived in and around the village of St. Just for centuries. These kindly, hardworking souls were miners and devotedly religious churchgoers and some were even clergy. Being that they were solid

Methodists this also meant that there was no smoking, drinking, card playing or dancing either. And so I asked her once again about our Cornish relations, and again came the familiar stories about their virtues... and then prompted by this pirate party invite, I said something like..."Yes, but you didn't tell us about the pirates". Silence. And then, "Oh well yes, and the smugglers; and our women were in on it, as well ! People were poor, you understand, and those looted ships carried silk and lace, as well as tea, saffron, brandy and tobacco".

Now our family was becoming much more interesting. I shared this information with my daughter, who had no idea about these colorful people in her past; she enjoyed her party and the treasure hunt, which had something to do with a hidden stash of chocolate and I didn't give much more thought to this incident. In my mind, at that time, this information came through my only daughter, rather than one of my sons, due to the women's involvement with the silks and lace, since some of these relations were milliners.

The Field, however, had another surprise waiting for me in Germany. Several years later, I was in Munich offering a seminar on second generation war trauma on the 50th anniversary of the Allied Invasion of Normandy. Interestingly, six of us present had fathers in the later, Italian Battle of Anzio which was quite a synchronicity in itself. And yet, there was more; given that one of our participants was British and in knowing my last name, had brought along a Cornish newspaper describing the anniversary celebrations in St. Just. Afterward, as I took some time to read through this edition, I was startled by a lengthy article about lady pirates. Cornish lady pirates!

My daughter was excited with this news and eager to tell her friends and I knew that I now had some serious research to do. As it turns out, female pirates have existed throughout history and are not all that rare, and there even exists a **Pirate Queens Coloring Book.**

Given that there is ample literature on this subject I was able to narrow my attention to lady pirates in

Cornwall, specifically in the St. Just, Penwith District, to see what I could find out about them in the context of Cornish culture; and what that may have to do with any hidden dynamics within my family system. I have been to the Duchy of Cornwall, located near Land's End; (the first, last and most westerly area in the U.K. Mainland), and St. Just in particular; many times since my first visit at age 21. After college, I traveled there to visit my Great Aunt Lucy Angwin, who was our last family member to reside in the ancient stone cottage along Victoria Row.

Ours was a gentle time of long, quiet walks on narrow paths, along nearby and familiar cliffs overlooking the sea; followed by a tea with freshly baked scones lathered with thick, yellowish Cornish cream, topped with freshly gathered wild blackberries, found along our way. Evenings were passed by a warm coal fire, while poring over a number of very old family photographs. One foggy morning, we traveled by way of a rickety old rural bus toward Penzance, to a bookstore where she gifted me with several classic novels involving

Cornish history; Daphne du Maurier novels and so forth....and then we enjoyed more tea and scones in a nearby café. Sadly, I was much too young to fully appreciate her generosity, especially now that I am more than a decade older than my "elderly" relation was then.

While my mother was born in the USA, she grew up along Victoria Row and went to school there in St. Just. Early on, I realized that my American Mother was "homesick" with longing for someplace else. Later on, I learned that this was even more the case with her mother, who crossed the Atlantic many times, and finally, at the end, my Grandfather took her ashes "home". During my last visit "home", I had an opportunity to spend some time with Mother's childhood friends, then in their late eighties and early nineties.."There are Cornish", Mother used to say, "who will tell you that they have never been to England". As strange as this may seem, the Cornish consider themselves no more English than the Irish, Welsh or Scots and they maintain an ongoing tribal antipathy toward Londoners and other outsiders, tax-collectors and the EU.

It could be that a deeply-rooted Cornish sense of non-English separateness, has some geographic basis in the fact that their rocky peninsula is surrounded on three sides by the sea, with the fourth boundaried by the River Tamar that divides this West Country duchy, (nearly sea to sea), from England.

Cornwall's mostly agreeable climate is made possible by a proximity to the Gulf Stream which provides ample moisture, by way of frequent "mizzles" (mists+drizzle), and mild temperatures that usually warm at least two months ahead of the rest of Britain.

The Cornish language, closely related to Welsh and ancient Breton dialects, is enjoying a revival and is reflected throughout the landscape, in place names and many words, similar to Welsh, with an abundance of barely pronounceable consonants and a scarcity of vowels.

The monochrome simplicity of the Cornish flag; white cross on a black field, looks to me, at least, like a smoothed out abstraction of that grinning "Jolly Roger" skull and cross bones flag flown aboard pirate vessels. This familiar image brings a sly smile of recognition now that I have come to understand the historical importance, and perhaps necessity for piracy and smuggling for the survival needs of an impoverished population of Celtic tribal folk. Cornwall remains the poorest county in Britain, still populated by those who have long felt themselves to be over-taxed and otherwise oppressed by the corrupt minions of the British Empire.

While the Cornish economy depended upon fishing, hard-scrabble farming and mining; these resources were undependable for many reasons, including sudden sea and weather changes. When ore veins ran out, as they often did, local tin and copper mines abruptly closed, leaving workers with few other resources. Some immigrated, as did my grandfather; others starved or turned to "alternative economies", which included poaching, smuggling, piracy and other survival-related disciplines. These often desperate situations have been recently dramatized in a marvelous remake of the **Poldark** mini-series, based on the epic Cornish novels of Winston Graham.

The dire circumstances of the Cornish economy were such that, piracy and smuggling operations became integral to their insular culture, to the degree that even clergy were involved. Contraband could be hidden in church crypts, bell towers, pulpits and tombs. (cornishlinks.co.uk). Almost all coastal towns had some connection to smuggling, and still this was dangerous business, and penalties were harsh. Since these contraband operations were sometimes carried out quite openly, town folk took to a studied practice of "watching the wall".

Kipling wrote about this in his *Smuggler's Song:*

"*Them that ask no questions, isn't told a lie*
Watch the wall, my darling, while the gentlemen go by".

Therefore, if smugglers were arrested, villagers could truthfully testify that they had seen nothing, for hearing was not considered evidence. As a result, there developed a culture within which "everyone knows and no one says", and information is necessarily withheld from any and all outsiders.

Smugglers also contrived and promoted ghost-stories and other scary tall-tales in order to keep any curious away from places important to their clandestine activities. This was not difficult given the territory's otherworldly landscape and the long-standing traditions having to do with the mysterious and paranormal. This region abounds in moorlands of heather and gorse and is said to be riddled with dangerous peat bogs and "piskies", small mischievous sprites, who are given to confuse the unwary wanderer, who soon becomes "lost". Ugly troll-like spriggans are believed to inhabit old ruins, guarding buried treasure (or contraband) and also acting as fairy guards. While brownies are generally considered to be helpful household spirits; if not appeased, they could turn spiteful and things begin to disappear. Miners believed in noisy "Knockers", heard from the eerie depths of underground tunnels, that warn of impending danger; and these underground spirits also needed to be appeased, or else.

Cornwall's ancient landscape also abounds with tall standing stones and circles, and holy wells sacred since pagan times. These small, rural springs are associated with the ability to grant wishes and heal. Visitors attach small strips of cloth or "clouthies" to branches of nearby trees to represent their plea. Coastal regions, that travel-agents extol as the Cornish Riviera, are as treacherous as they are beautiful, given the often ferocious winds, monstrous waves, changeable cross-currents and tides; as well as sharp cliffs and jagged rocks hidden by rolling sheets of sea fog. For the impoverished locals, this perilous configuration offered opportunity, as well as danger.

As my Mother explained, desperation was conducive to plunder; and shipwrecks along the Cornish coast were not uncommon. Whatever washed up along these treacherous shores was considered to be common property. According to British law, it was illegal to plunder any wrecked ship as long as there were any survivors aboard. This technicality has led to stories of unfortunate survivors having drowned just as rescue boats arrived from a nearby shore.

We have even darker tales of "wreckers", made famous in Daphne Du Maurier's West Country Gothic novel, **Jamaica Inn.** These clandestine gangs traveled by night and used false light-signals in order to deliberately lure ships onto hidden rocks; and then helped themselves to the spoils. Nowadays, these stories of professional wreckers are considered to be mostly fiction.

In view of this recently discovered information about a cultural interdependence of pirates, smugglers and complicit clergy and town folk; it seems that the career of Cornwall's most notorious lady pirates involved all three of these elements. In times of war and other hardship, occupations previously held by men were taken over, by necessity, by women. These were also times when some women had to dress as men in order to seek employment. However, these were apparently neither the situations nor motivation underlying the stories of Cornwall's most notable, 16th century female pirates; both members of the Killigrew family.

Elizabeth Trewinnard, (1530–1570) also known as Lady Mary Killigrew, was an unconventional aristocrat, daughter of a Suffolk pirate, whose husband was a former pirate, made Vice Admiral by Elizabeth I and tasked with suppressing piracy. It seems that her ladyship enjoyed sailing adventures; and when her husband was away at sea, Lady Mary engaged in piracy, using her staff at Arwenack Manor, located in an area which is now Falmouth. Lady Mary Killigrew is rumored to have served as inspiration for the dominant character in the novel: **The Grove of Eagles** by Winston Graham, there described as a woman who "knew all she wanted and wanted all she knew". She was reportedly arrested for piracy, receiving stolen goods, and sentenced to death until pardoned by the Queen who may have realized that the skills of the Killigrew family could well serve as her privateers in times of war. (Anne Wallace Sharp, **Daring Pirate Women,** 2002)

Lady Mary Killigrew's story is often confused or at least conflated with that of Lady Elizabeth Killigrew (1570s-1582) whose piracy related operations were based at Pendennis Castle in Falmouth Harbor. Lady Elizabeth is also said to have been arrested and then pardoned for similar reasons as Lady Mary. Given the Cornish penchant for tall-tales and secrecy, it is difficult to clearly sort out exactly who was involved and what actually went on. While I have no information as to any direct connection to those highly adventurous Killigrews, Cornwall was and is sparsely populated, and my ancestors were there in the region from the 12th century onward.

In modern times, Mother's family still maintains a very keen sense of when they feel that it is maybe sometimes best to "look to the wall", and the tradition of "everyone knows what is not being said" continues. At a recent family gathering with four generations of Cornish cousins, for example, our dinner conversation was ostensibly about the quality of the local seafood. Being Cornish, we were of course communicating about something else entirely, in this instance, the fact that family members having babies "out of wedlock" is nothing new in our system and therefore should not be a topic of undue concern. In the absence of dissent, we were able to move along to dessert without incident.

This long tradition of secrecy and distrust of outsiders, apparently rooted in the Cornish pirate and smuggling culture, persisted well into my Mother's generation. One of our family's strictly enforced rules was that no one was ever to discuss anything relating to the family outside of the house, ever. Mother is the youngest of six and her parent's families and their parent's families were even larger. Our family events involved many relatives, several generations and a multitude of cousins, second cousins and cousins "once or twice removed "; and just maybe a few "wood pile relations", as well. While their status was never really defined, it was somehow understood that these people belonged with us…"somehow".

Growing up, I didn't think to find it strange, that while we often had visitors, never was there anyone who was not a relative; and rarely an overnight guest. While my Mother and her husband socialized at church and civic events, all holidays and vacation times were spent only with our relations at their various guest cottages along the New Jersey Shore. As a teenager I was allowed to have friends over to our house, but never to stay overnight. While my step-father remained distant, Mother was always gracious and still visibly "uncomfortable" until my friends left. Absolutely no one was welcome to arrive without due notice and even relatives knew not to ever, ever, "just drop by".

As a retired marriage and family therapist, I have since learned that insular, secretive families such as our ancient Celtic clan, that have "secrets" dating far back into historical times, are now viewed with suspicion. While I do not disagree, as to the import of family secrets, not all are necessarily destructive nor pathological, and many have served as a vital resource in overall survival strategies. Moreover, much of such apparently insular and seemingly secretive behaviors have ancestral roots, deserving of respect.

This Cornish insularity was balanced by my father's family, who are French, and very social, "artsy", fond of travel, interesting company, and loving of intrigue and good gossip. While mother's clan was patriarchal, Father's was and is a matriarchal system and I feel that I have deeply benefited from the contrast. I was reminded of my Cornish genes recently as one of my translators explained why my English writing style is so difficult to translate into any kind of direct literal sense. "Your true meaning", she offered, "is often implied, somewhere in between the lines ", and this is likely true. And yes, there is still this restlessness and longing for the Old World; the U.K. and Cornwall, especially.

And so, at this point, it seems that this ancestral treasure hunt for clues has revealed nothing all that dramatic, as directly relates to either my daughter's or my life, so far, and still we now have a deeper understanding of certain aspects of our complex heritage. If in fact, there is something else of importance that we really need to know, The Field will likely come up with another clue; and meanwhile, I will just have to wait.

Orthorexia: Really?

"The smart way to keep people passive and obedient it to strictly limit the spectrum of acceptable opinion, but allow very lively debate within that spectrum". (Noam Chomsky, **The Common Good,** 1998)

"The food you eat can be either the safest and most powerful form of medicine or slowest form of poison". (Ann Wigmore)

"Eat food, not too much, mostly plants". (Michael Pollan, **The Omnivore's Dilemma**)

"It is no measure of health to be well adjusted to a profoundly sick society". (Jiddu Krishnamurti)

Among the rising tide of Orwellian dis-info, we now find the message that eating right is now wrong and probably even pathological. (health = sick) Step away from that locally grown, organic produce, now, …or else! OK, so what is really going on here? *Orthorexia nervosa* is being proposed as the latest addition to a growing lexicon of dodgy diagnoses listed in the American Psychiatric Association's **Diagnostic and Statistical Manual (DSM 5),** the so called "Bible" recommended to mental health professionals. By way of disclosure, as a retired health and mental health professional, you may want to know that I have found this eminently weighty volume to be exactly the right size and weight to serve as an improvised door stop. While it has been considered by many to represent a valuable classification and diagnostic tool, the DSM series has come under increasing, well deserved, criticism. Just recently, we find that the DSM's politically saturated task force have admitted to collaborative relationships among government, academia and industry elements vital to development of pharmacological treatment for mental disorders. (David J. Kupfer M.D., DSM-V Task Force Member Disclosure Report, May 2, 2011).

If approved, *Orthorexia* would take its place among a lexicon of dubious diagnostic categories such as: Disruptive Mood Disorder (temper tantrums), Oppositional Defiant Disorder (Two Year Olds, Adolescence, Social Activism, Political Dissidents, Alternative Media, most cats), Major Depressive Disorder (normal grief, Basset Hounds), Adult Attention Deficit Disorder (boredom), Minor Neuro-cognitive Disorder (Senior Moments) General Anxiety Disorder (Everyday Worries), to cite just a few eligible for medication and other allopathic treatments. Fortunes will soon be made with the advent of state-mandated compulsory vaccinations, for these hypothetical, and other real or cynically fabricated conditions; if this dystopic trend of medical fascism is allowed to continue. *Orthorexia nervosa* (health food eating disorder) is named for the Greek *ortho* meaning "straight, proper or correct" by American doctor Steven Bratman, who claims that he developed an unhealthy obsession with eating "proper food" during his time at a rural commune and was "seduced by righteous eating". This complaint sounded sufficiently serious to a group of Italian researchers, who then developed an ORTO-15 questionnaire with a cut off score of 40+ signifying *Orthorexia,* for sure. (pathological eating behavior). Given that I both love cats and enjoy just a touch of self-diagnosed Oppositional Defiant Disorder, I have refused to take this test. Still, I find these research results interesting with their female-male ratio of two to one.

Most of these *Orthorexia* studies have been conducted within population sub-groups considered to be at risk, such as health care professionals. Turkish doctors, we learn, scored just above 40 and Turkish street performers a bit higher at 56.4 percent. Opera singers scored some 81.1 percent and Spanish yoga teachers, most at risk with 86 per cent. Some reassurance, depending upon your point of view, might be found in the fact that among Austrian dietitians, (using the Bratman test, yet another questionnaire), only 12.8 percent could be classified as *Orthorexic.* (Rebecca Reynolds, UK Daily Mail, April 10, 2015). I also find it interesting that these researchers excluded pregnant women and Olympic athletes from their studies since these sub-groups seems to be at serious risk given their likely concerns with healthy eating.

In contrast to this Orwellian nonsense, Dr. Joseph Mercola has taken an admirable, oppositional (defiant), stance against Monsanto's genetically modified Franken-food, and their power and control obsession with making anything natural into something synthetic and patented; hence becoming something akin to the Homeland Security of Food. Never mind the fact that **Roundup,** Monsanto's number one herbicide, has been recently outed as a likely cause of cancer. (Jon Rapport, Activist Post, April 15, 2015) :

…the United States Department of Agriculture (USDA) has taken the position that organic farming, such as free range chickens, live stock and non-GMO seeds that they cannot control are potential security threats. USDA has even begun   putting in writing, directives on how they can keep organic farming 'contained' (Mercola: (September 17, 2012).

Undaunted, Dr. Mercola and others continue to warn about the consequences of consuming dangerous amounts of sugar. In the eyes of our corporate controllers this dangerous situation is now becoming acute with an increasing number of courageous awake and aware farmers, at considerable personal and financial risk, currently banding together to embrace non-GMO products. Even worse, several major mainstream grocery outlets such as Safe-Way, mindful of customer demands, who vote with their checkbooks, have added an impressive array of organic and non-GMO products. Whole Foods and other health oriented chains, catering to potential *orthorexics* are also doing very well.

I resonate with **Zen Gardner** and am a regular follower of his ongoing web site blogs laden with sane advice for those of us in search of any kind of relative balance in the face of increasing oppression. Zen advises, in his "Junk Food Habit" (February 18, 2015) that junk foods are OK, once in awhile, given the reality that our cravings are induced by highly addictive additives as elements in a not so slow genocide for profit and control. Here one might consider a possible reality that these fast foods mostly appeal to our poor, overly stressed and their children. Zen postulates that this toxic spew of tasty ingredients have the potential to cause near-permanent changes within our brain's reward circuitry, that might also trigger obesity... and who knows what else. Moreover, according to Zen, we are under an overarching attack by complicit government, and multinational corporations shamelessly hawking GMO's, adulterated foods, vaccines, pharmaceuticals, atmospheric aerosols, genetic alterations and the like. Powerful minions, more interested in weakening and subjugating humanity via health de-gradation, dumbed-down education, mindless "bread and circus" government controlled mega-corporate media, depraved violence and sex oriented entertainment, together with a series of draconian crackdowns by an increasingly militarized police force. (Zen Gardner, May 2015)

The World Health Organization estimates that at least 2.8 million die every year from diseases linked to obesity, heart disease, diabetes or stroke. In plain language, their findings indicate that Franken-food habits are killing 40% more people than war, famine, dictatorships, murders and politicians can put together. These facts alone, offer an entirely new dimension into the study of social, collective trauma and genocidal, de-population agendas. (Zen, February 19, 2015)

And still, as Michael Pollan describes, thanks to a succession of awful farm bills, vicious tactics and flaccid USDA rules, many American farmers are currently paid to grow massive quantities of (inedible) GMO corn. There is some good news in reports that a record number of these farmers are now switching to non-GMO crops in 2015. While this may sound encouraging, the controllers have stepped up a nationwide campaign against those defiant foodies who prefer to grow their own fruits and vegetables, by outlawing their modest home garden plots as "violations of community standards".

As dark as this may seem, there may be a glimmer of hope on the horizon. MacDonald's sales are steadily decreasing and they have even had to leave Iceland due to lack of revenue. Should you find yourself in Reykjavik, you may want to visit the last Big Mac with cheese and chips now located in the country's National Food Museum, nicely displayed, with no preservatives needed, under glass.

MAY

Spirit of Place: Tlatelolco

"The spirit of place is a strange thing. Our mechanical age tries to override it. But it does not succeed. In the end, the strange, sinister spirit of place…will smash our mechanical oneness to smithereens – and all that we think. The real thing will go off with a pop, and we shall be left staring."   (D.H. Lawrence)

"The city is not just a geographical or spatial place. It is an essential process of our lives and our history. The city is us and where we come from. To take back the space of the city is to recover for all of us a territory that transcribes our lives". (Cuauhtemoc Cardenas, First elected Mayor of Mexico City)

"Ideology always leads to violence". (Terrance McKenna)

In the Old World's classical religions, the concept of *genius loci* referred to a presiding deity or "spirit of place". Now in the New World and in contemporary cultures, the term refers more to a location's distinct place-ness than its past; its current and future essence, rather than a necessarily protective entity. In keeping with Rupert Sheldrake's research into morphogenetic fields, and his notion that places also have "fields of memory" that often have to do with unresolved trauma, it seems that Mexico City's Tlatelolco provides an interesting case in point.

Also known as Xaltelolco, which translates from Nahuatl, known informally as Aztec, as "little hill of the land". Tlatelolco is located in an area of the Cuauhtemoc borough of Mexico City and centered upon the Plaza de las Tres Culturas. The three cultures that are represented in this plaza are from the Pre-Colombian Aztecs, who called themselves Mexicas; the Spanish Catholic, conquering colonizers; and a modern office and Nuevo Leon housing complex of contemporary "Mestizo" culture of the independent nation.

This district of Mexico City which arose as a Pre-Colombian city state, was eventually taken over by the ascendant Aztecs who commandeered this territory as part of their empire during the 13th century. The site subsequently became a setting for tribal warfare; and a partially excavated temple site has revealed practices of ritual torture, human sacrifice and a market in slave trade.

During the Spanish conquest, a war between the *Conquistadors* and the Aztecs in 1531 resulted in the slaughter of some 40,000 Aztec men, women and children, thought to have taken place in one single day. The deaths from this battle, which was in truth a massacre, left a deep scar within the collective psyche of the newly established colony. Centuries later a plaque was set up on the site that reads: "The battle was not a triumph, nor was it a defeat. It was the painful birth of the *Mestizo* nation that is the Mexico of today".

After the Spanish conquest, the Aztec temple dedicated to their War God Huitzilipochthli was demolished and the plaza re-named Santiago de Tlatelolco after the militant Spanish patron Saint James, whose mythic crushing of the Moors was widely credited with the subsequent victory of the Latin American conquest. Building-stones and other ruins from the War God's temple were used in the construction of the Franciscan Church of Santiago de Tlatelolco commissioned by Hernan Cortes in 1524. It stands there to this day, together with the

remains of a Franciscan convent. (<u>colonial-</u>
<u>mexico.com</u>)

Tlatelolco's age-old, violent fractal of conquest,
destruction, repression, and bloodshed has
continued on through several more iterations in
modern times with no end in sight. In 1968 the
government was preparing to host the Olympic
Games, as an opportunity to elevate the stature of a
prosperous and stable Mexico in the eyes of the
global community. In opposition, a coalition of leftist
high school and college students sought to use this
same opportunity to bring attention to their country's
social ills; especially the violent overreach of police
and military against the citizenry. The students were
also demanding immediate release of classmates
jailed in previous protests. In response, the Mexican
government prepared an Olympic Battalion; a
paramilitary squad to insure that protesters would
not be able to interrupt the games.

The confrontations began on October 2nd, 1968 as
protesters gathered at the Plaza de las Tres
Culturas for an afternoon rally, 10 days before the

opening ceremonies. At the same time, that activists gathered, snipers from the battalion assumed strategic posts up on the Nuevo Leon housing complex, which gave them a clear view of the citizens below. During these peaceful protests, the Mexican army and the police infiltrated the crowd and blocked off all of the exits from the square.

Although no one is certain where the first shot came from, (likely from an agent provocateur), at 6:10 PM the Plaza became a living hell; and yet another massacre occurred. Other security forces joined in and fleeing protesters were easy targets with as many 300 to 2,000 killed, (exact numbers remain unknown), and many others were wounded, arrested and "disappeared". This Night of Tlatelolco has left a lasting memory in Mexican politics and especially among the country's student population.

Two decades later, on September 9, 1985, these and other painful memories concerning this site re-surfaced with the 8.1 magnitude earthquake that caused major damage in Mexico City. The Tlatelolco Complex was hit particularly hard as two of the

Nuevo Leon housing units collapsed, killing all of the residents inside. This tragedy was made even more painful by the revelation that this collapse was exacerbated by a lethal combination of illegal cost-cutting during construction and lack of proper maintenance. The final toll was somewhere between 200 and 300 fatalities. Due to earthquake damage, eight other buildings in the complex had to be demolished and four more had their upper floors removed. A persistent aura of danger remains, as poor maintenance continues and this high crime area is under virtual curfew by nightfall. (Drew Reed, theguardian.com, May 2015).

The latest iteration in the Tlatelolco fractal occurred in the September 26th disappearance of 43 leftist student teachers from the Raul Isidro Burgos Normal Rural School of Ayotzinapa in Tixla. They were part of a bus convoy headed for Mexico City to demonstrate on the anniversary of the October 2, 1968 Night of Tlatelolco at the Plaza des Tres Culturas. These students were last seen in the custody of police, government security, and army personnel in Iguala.

As of now, the official government story is that the local drug cartels were responsible for the kidnapping and cremation of the students in a garbage dump in the town of Cocula, near to the abduction site. Locals scoff at this explanation given the fact that there was heavy rainfall all night on the date when this cremation supposedly took place. Funerary and other forensic experts maintain that a cremation of that many bodies would have required a degree of heat only possible in an indoor facility. Massive nation-wide protests have ensued with the incident remaining unresolved and thus likely to give rise to yet another cycle of violence.

Chernobyl's Fiery Field of Memory

"Show me a fantasy novel about Chernobyl – there isn't one. Because reality is more fantastic". (Svetlana Alexievich, **Voices From Chernobyl: The Oral History of a Nuclear Disaster)**

"The unleashed power of the atom has changed everything except our thinking. Thus we are drifting toward catastrophe beyond conception. We shall require a substantially new manner of thinking if mankind is to survive". (Albert Einstein)

"The nuclear industry is waging a war against humanity". (John Gofman, M.D. Ph.D. former Manhattan Project scientist and Associate Director Lawrence Nuclear Laboratory, U.C. Berkeley 1963-1969)

Social traumatologists, politicians, terrorists and the media, know that individual, family and social traumas tend to occur on the anniversary of previous and unresolved traumas. Over the years and in several of my books, I have explored biological researcher Rupert Sheldrake's idea that places also have "fields of memory" that can play a role in traumatic repetitions. One of those places is located in war-torn northern Ukraine, at the site of the damaged reactor Unit Four at the Chernobyl nuclear power station.

As the world now knows, (despite initial efforts of cover-up), while this area was still part of the former USSR, on April 25,1986, something went terribly wrong. For some reason, now lost to history, the site's nuclear engineers decided to turn off the safety systems in their un-contained reactor in order to "see what would happen". As a result, there was in fact a lot to see; which we will continue to see and feel, far into our foreseeable future and possibly even far beyond that. (St. Just, **Trauma: Time, Space and Fractals,** 2012).

A steam explosion, graphite fire and nuclear-meltdown event expelled a volcanic release of highly radioactive particles into our planetary atmosphere carrying levels of radiation 300 times greater than the fire-bombing of Hiroshima. As a result, those of us here and visiting within the entire Northern Hemisphere have been experiencing an ongoing, international, human and environmental catastrophe. During the immediate aftermath of this nuclear folly, more than 400,000 citizens in the nearby town of Pripyat were uprooted from their homes. With only three hours notice, these evacuees were unaware that they would never be able to return to what became a 30 km (18.6 miles) exclusion zone.

Over the course of the following summer, an unusually intense round of forest fires served to further a spread of highly radioactive isotopes. At the time, much of this catastrophe was new and unexpected since there had never before been a radiological disaster of this scale. Unfortunately, this nightmare scale has been necessarily updated. While Chernobyl ranked seven at the top of an existing scale for nuclear accidents, a new category was needed. Since the disaster at seaside Fukushima Daiichi far exceeded land-locked Chernobyl, with four damaged reactors, (three in meltdown), spewing ongoing leaks into the air, ocean and underground water supplies. Fukushima now seriously out-ranks Chernobyl with an intensity rating of eight. (enenews.com, August 13, 2012). Let us hope, pray and rise up in protest, so that there will never be the necessity to update this scale to anything like a nine or even a ten.

The site chosen for Ukraine's first nuclear power plant has a long, dark history of fiery death and destruction.

The plant was named for the nearby town of Chernobyl which dates from the 12th century onward, which was in turn, named for another kind of plant. In Ukrainian, the herb called *chornobyl* with the botanical term *Artemesia vulgaris* has been confused with its close cousin *Artemesia absinthium*, a bitter herb with medicinal properties use to flavor absinthe and vermouth, also known as wormwood. Mary Mycio, addresses this confusion in her "In Wormwood Forest" (September 9, 2005), since both herbs are common to the Chernobyl region.

Shortly after the 1986 disaster a religious meme appeared warning that the name Chernobyl translates to wormwood, thus fulfilling biblical prophesies in the Book of Revelation; as this herb is a frequent biblical symbol for bitterness, calamity and sorrow. In reality, the Russianized Chernobyl from the Ukrainian *chornobyl*, translates as "mugwort" and not it's botanical cousin wormwood. In Medieval Europe mugwort was used as a protective charm.

Prior to the 20th century, the Chernobyl region was inhabited by Ukrainian and Polish peasants and a relatively large number of Jews. The Jewish population suffered greatly from fiery pogroms where whole villages were burned to cinders and inhabitants raped, beaten, kidnapped and slaughtered. These pogroms were especially severe in 1905 and again from 1919-1920. The region also suffered from mass killings during Stalin's ruthless collectivization campaign and the horrendous famine that followed.

The local Polish community was forcibly deported to Kazakhstan in 1936 during Stalin's Frontier Clearance. The Chernobyl region was also the site of some of the most heinous Nazi atrocities in 1941 and was occupied by the German army until 1943, during which time the entire Jewish population was systematically murdered. (Norman Davies, **Europe: A History,** 1996).

In the years since the April 1986 nuclear disaster, the highly contaminated surrounding forests have been subjected to a series of fires due to climate change and drought in 1992, 2002, 2008 and now in 2015. Extensive woodland death due to radiation has created an excess of tinder with dry leaves, and trees that desiccate but do not decay, thus giving rise to further nuclear devastation via radioactive wildfires. These dying, mostly pine, plantations, surrounding the exclusion zone, cannot be decontaminated and are considered to be too dangerous and expensive to clear. (Kevin Kamps, **Russian Insider**, May 6, 2015). When ignited, they spread deadly radioisotopes through smoking foliage, pine needles and cones along with airborn pollens, which continue to cycle through the planetary ecosystem.

This latest iteration in Chernobyl's long fiery fractal of destruction, erupted with yet another wildfire that broke out in April, 2015, exactly on the 29th anniversary of the initial fire and explosion. Arson is suspected in view of the date and the fact that this conflagration broke out on both sides of the nearby River Vuhz. While information was hard to come by, for political and other logistical reasons; satellite images revealed that tree-top flames and strong winds combined to enable a rapid spread of wildfire over some 10,000 hectares of contaminated areas around and within the exclusion zone. As the fire spread toward the power plant's crippled installations, flames reportedly came within 3 miles of buried nuclear waste. (enenews.com, April 29,

2015).

Ukrainian police, National Guard and fire-fighting units were all on high alert while government officials insisted that everything was under control. Such a statement is hardly credible given video footage of the brave front-line firefighters manually batting down radioactive flames, with sparse equipment and many without any protective gear. Nevertheless, it was announced that these exclusion-zone fires were out in early May, without mention of still-smoldering, airborne, potentially death-dealing smoke.

As Scientific Secretary of the European Committee on Radiation Risks, Dr. Christopher Busby explains: The potential danger in this fire comes from radioactive contaminants that these now burning plant materials have absorbed through a process of bio-accumulation. At least some deadly contaminates would have been incorporated into the woods. In other words, they land on the ground in 1986 and they get absorbed into the trees, plants and then all of the biosphere. And when they burn, toxins just become re-suspended. It's like Chernobyl all over again. All of that material that fell on the ground will now be burned up into the air and available for people, and all living things, to breathe and absorb. (rt.com, April 2015). The exact trajectory of the latest, fire generated radioactive plume, will depend upon which way the winds blow and these can be expected to circle our planet every 40 days or so. Residents downwind from the immediate fallout are advised to remain indoors and avoid contact with subsequent rainfall. The unfortunate truth remains that Chernobyl's latest wildfire crisis is a natural part of what is now a centuries-long disaster cycle which will continue to repeat over and again.

The crippled Unit Four reactor continues to leak lethal toxins; and that hastily built sarcophagus, currently in place, is seriously cracked and rapidly deteriorating. Efforts to replace this faltering containment structure have stalled due to lack of funding and Ukraine's political unrest and instability. If and when this massive new structure is completed and in place, it too will have to be replaced, because the radionuclides will remain dangerous, in some cases, for tens of thousands or hundreds of thousands of years. As long as we have these long-lived hot particles, they will simply cycle through our planetary ecosystem and be taken up by plants and other living things and then released through fires for further and ongoing deadly recycle.

So now, Ukrainian officials, dutifully reading from the (by now, all too familiar and spurious, international, nuclear- industry) playbook script, assure all concerned that this fire is out, problem solved, radiation levels are not increased in the affected area and there has been and will be no danger to human health. (Please go back to sleep). If you are reading this blog, chances are that you have heard these self-serving bromides parroted by the minions of this much too powerful, death-dealing, nuclear industry. To add to the insult of our collective intelligence, there is a nuclear industry-funded YouTube documentary, gone viral, purporting that the radioactive Chernobyl exclusion zone has become a kind of idyllic wildlife renewal refuge. As long as a trusting public is willing to swallow this toxic swill, these death-dealing, time-bomb, perpetual-death machines will continue to infest and threaten our planet.

It is well beyond time for us to face the fact that nuclear

power, in any form, is not and never was "safe", clean, nor inexpensive. Such Neo-Orwellian statements have been categorically proven to be utterly false and diabolically manipulative. Moreover, it is my conviction that no technology that has been weaponized can ever, truly be either life-positive or "safe". Instead of holding clandestine symposiums about how to "safely" dispose of our deadly nuclear waste, how about similar energies being invited to explore that self-destructive mind-set that found it somehow necessary to create these death-dealing, radioactive horrors ?

Probably it is not news that our current, life threatening predicament has to do with a misguided, anti-life, mindset that created these nuclear threats to all life upon our planet, and that any far reaching solutions are absolutely not to be found anywhere within the realm of any military, industrial, or energy, magnates. Perhaps it is too much to hope for, in these increasingly dark and difficult times, and still I have a persistent vision that there exists, now or somewhere in our near future, something like an alchemical technology that has the ability to transform these deadly nuclear particles into a more life-positive form. And, I also feel, that this will not be possible until we can find a way to choose and authentically embrace a more peaceful and inclusive frame of consciousness toward ourselves, each other and all living things. Meanwhile, to whatever degree possible, it is probably best to stay out of the rain.

JUNE

Trauma and Relationship: Hannah Arendt and Martin Heidegger

"We are so accustomed to the old opposition of reason and and passion, of mind and life, that the idea of passionate thinking, in which passionate thinking and being alive become one, can be a bit startling". (Hannah Arendt: "Martin Heidegger is Eighty Years Old", 1969)

"He who thinks great thoughts often makes great errors". (Martin Heidegger)

"Love has reasons which reason cannot understand". (Blaise Pascal, Philosopher, 1623-1662)

Relatively recent revelations concerning a passionate and clandestine love affair between two of the most prominent intellectual giants of the 20th century, political theorist Hannah Arendt and German philosopher Martin Heidegger, is likely to challenge an image of Heidegger as an austere and abstract thinker and of Arendt as a consummately independent, self-assured, personality. Martin Heidegger (1889-1976) was a seminal thinker within the fields of existential phenomenology and philosophical hermeneutics, best known for his ground breaking **Being in Time** (1927). This masterwork, deeply rooted in both Eastern mysticism and German Romantic tradition is widely considered to be one of the most influential philosophical works of the 20th century. (Elzbieta Ettinger, **Hannah Arendt. Martin Heidegger**, 1995).

Johanna "Hannah" Arendt (1906-1975) a secular Jew born in East Prussia, within a thoroughly assimilated, leftist and economically comfortable family, was one the 20th century's greatest and most original political theorists. While she has also been characterized as a philosopher, she made clear her distrust of the pure thinking of philosophy as isolated from moral and political judgment. Among her many writings was the first major work, **The Origins of Totalitarianism** (1951), followed by **The Human Condition, Men in Dark Times,** and the highly contentious **Eichmann in Jerusalem: A Report on the Banality of Evil** (1963); recently featured in the German film, **Hannah Arendt** (2012) directed by Margarethe von Trotta.

Both Heidegger and Arendt were highly controversial figures in relation to their personal and professional lives as well as their vastly different responses to events during and after the multiple horrors of the

Third Reich. Heidegger was an avid, unrepentant Nazi and Arendt an anti-fascist refugee and lifelong supporter of Jewish causes, and still they maintained an unlikely bond which lasted for more than 40 years during some of the darkest moments of 20th century history. Hostile critics of both scholars have sought to dismiss, trivialize, condemn, and even presume to diagnose their relationship as a result of childhood trauma, psycho-pathology, (victim/perpetrator bond), a study in denial, morally reprehensible, adulterous, perverse (sado-masochistic Jewish submission to manipulative Aryan master) and all in all, a sad sordid affair. (Judith Shulevitz, NY Times, January 10,1995). Many of these dubious judgments have since been held out as evidence that none of their intellectual achievements are worthy of further study.

This is not so surprising given our human proclivity to attempt to exclude, pathologize and even persecute any and all of that which does not fit comfortably within our often, narrowly defined, politically generated, consensus reality. In contrast, I would offer the possibility that even the word "relationship" might prove inadequate to describe the depth of this admittedly mysterious bond, which is in itself, worthy of study for those of us interested in social trauma, relatedness, and our all too Human Condition.

We begin in 1924, when at the age of 18, Hannah Arendt, a strikingly beautiful German of Jewish origin appeared as a devoted student in intensely charismatic Professor Martin Heidegger's philosophy class at Marburg University at a time when he was a rising superstar in prestigious academic circles. Heidegger initiated their affair and they quickly became lovers. Secrecy was imperative given that Heidegger was a married father of two sons. His wife Elfride, a zealous Nazi and outspoken anti-Semite, had recently had an affair of her own, resulting in the birth of a second son Hermann, which Heidegger, to his credit, took as his own. This passionate liaison between teacher and student continued on for four years, during which Hannah made herself available to him anytime and anywhere that he so designated. (Daniel Maier-Katkin, **Stranger From Abroad,** 2010)

Those with a modern day feminist perspective have been highly critical of Arendt's "slavish" devotion to her mentor. Yet, her apparent obedience and passivity cannot be judged by modern day standards and was quite consistent within the norms of behavior for students at German universities who related to their professors as masters. The professor literally stood upon a pedestal, classroom atmospheres were solemn, etiquette obligatory and rules for conduct, dress, manners and appearances strictly observed. Small wonder that Arendt experienced a degree of culture shock, 30 years later, when she arrived as a visiting professor at the U.C. Berkeley campus among our often unkempt and easy going students; and the give and take of classroom discussions felt completely alien. (Ettinger, 1995)

Heidegger's affair with Hannah was a serious risk to his professional reputation and image of respectability; and in time, with fear of discovery and public scandal, he began to distance. A distraught Arendt left Marburg for Heidelberg in order to complete her dissertation; later published as **Augustine and Love,** with Karl Jaspers. While Hannah had left Marburg, she did not leave Heidegger and contact and letters continued on until his last letter before 1950, (written in 1933), sarcastically denying her suspicions and the widespread rumors of his anti-Semitism. Nevertheless, the facts are such that when Heidegger was appointed as Rector of the University of Freiburg, he joined the Nazi party, and lectured while wearing Brown Shirt, thus lending his considerable academic prestige to Hitler's cause.

Soon thereafter, Heidegger zealously purged this venerable institution of Jewish faculty and students. Moreover, records reveal, that he closely collaborated with Gestapo agents during their investigations of his colleagues, suspected of communist sympathies. Many of his former friends and colleagues were rendered almost speechless by this treachery, including his elderly Jewish mentor Edmund Husserl who had regarded Martin almost as a son. (Elizabeth Young-Bruehl, **Hannah Arendt: For Love Of The World,** 1982)

Hannah Arendt barely escaped the Holocaust and after a brief arrest and imprisonment by the Gestapo, followed by a period of internment in France, immigrated to America and finally broke off contact with Heidegger. Enraged and confused by his having embraced the Nazi cause, she blamed his ambitious careerism and Elfride's negative influence. In time, she even called Heidegger "a potential murderer" and then decided to take back those words. Now married to Marxist scholar, Heinrich Bluecher, a German refugee like herself; both brought their nightmares into exile and these nightmares brought them close. Bleucher understood love as "a galvanizing physical and spiritual force that also required that partners leave open spaces for each other to develop, act, and create", he wrote in 1937, "and so will I" and as such, agreed to be faithful only "in his own fashion". (Maier-Katkin, 2010)

In spite of her growing success as an international and influential public intellectual, Arendt suffered from her long estrangement from Heidegger; and with Bluecher's encouragement decided to initiate contact. During a post -war visit to Freiburg, she sent an unsigned note on hotel stationary summoning him and he came immediately for their meeting. In her words "it was as though we spoke to one another...for the first time in our lives". Martin was still Martin, his actions were despicable and still she recognized his humanity and admired his genius. Deeply moved by the profound honesty inherent within their reconciliation, upon returning home Heidegger, notorious for lying about just about everything, finally confessed to his wife that Hannah Arendt had been "the passion of his life" and inspiration for his work. Elfride responded with a jealous rage forbidding further contact... to no avail.

Eventually Frau Heidegger swallowed her pride and allowed the relationship as she realized that it was essential for her husband's well being. Heidegger was suffering from ill health and a nervous breakdown, and something like a depression in 1946, with both of their sons interned in Soviet prisoner of war camps, under very harsh conditions. Elfride also hoped that Hannah's prestige could deliver him from disgrace brought about in de-Nazification programs, wherein Brown Shirts were now out, and Heidegger was forbidden to teach. (Maier-Katkin, 2010).

At risk, and with some damage to her reputation, Hannah did lobby for Heidegger's academic rehabilitation and was widely questioned and criticized for having "forgiven Heidegger". In reality, this delicate process between them was not one of forgiveness, since Heidegger never apologized for any of his actions nor ever recanted his allegiance to the Nazi party. Moreover, Arendt felt that forgiveness produces an imbalance within a relationship, whereby the forgiver claims the moral high-ground and thus a separation remains. Recently, Bert Hellinger's systemic teachings have affirmed this reality.

For Heidegger and Arendt, their reconciliation came about through a mutual willingness to understand. While one can never truly know what really transpires within an intimate relationship, it does seem that these two high-powered public intellectuals who lived out their allegiances and consequences on opposing sides of the political spectrum, still managed to remain connected through an intensely private passion of the heart. For Arendt, love is inherently not only anti-political, but apolitical, and by its very nature unworldly. Empathy, passion and sympathy are not of this world, but reside within the realm of the heart. (T.G. Pavel, 1998). "The Heidegger Affair", MLN 103 (4):887-901). From this perspective, their unlikely bond serves as a clear testimony to the essential nature and power of love.

In 1961 Arendt traveled to Jerusalem serving as a self-appointed reporter for **The New Yorker,** as well as social critic, displaced person, witness and survivor. Her controversial coverage, and criticisms leveled against Zionism as a dangerous ethnocentric movement, the apparent collaboration of European Jewish Ghetto Councils (Judenräte) before and during the war, were not well received. In addition, many took offense at her criticism of some aspects of Israel's and Ben Gurion's theatrical conduct of the Eichmann trial, and the defendant whom she characterized as a "bland, non-descript, diligent, and not very intelligent bureaucrat ".

Hannah saw Eichmann as someone who personified neither hatred nor madness nor even an insatiable thirst for blood, but something far worse; the often faceless nature of evil itself, within a closed system run by psychopathic gangsters. Here she alleged, was Nazism (and totalitarianism) as it manifests as defined evil; as civic-norm and conventional goodness became something that wary survival-based, (go along, get along) citizens soon learned to ignore.

At that time, it seems that the collectively unaware assumed that such, even state-sponsored murders, were carried out by clearly identifiable, obviously demonic monsters. Arendt's unpopular perceptions to the contrary were validated by nearly everybody who attended the trials of mass killers after the war; and some defendants were actually respected doctors, pharmacists, nurses and so on. Many witnesses came away with some deeply disconcerting perceptions, that these monstrous mass murderers did not appear to differ in any way, from anyone else.

Those who doubt the accuracy of such perceptions might consider consulting Dr. Phililp Zimbardo's Stanford Prison Experiment, now a film; as well as Dr. Stanley Milgram's notorious experiments with ordinary people willing to inflict life threatening pain onto others, when ordered to do so by some "authority".

Arendt's, 1961 reportage quickly set off something like a civil-war among a number of public intellectuals.

Nevertheless, her prescient visions of inevitable and ongoing bloodshed between Israelis and Palestinians has indeed come to pass, with no immediate resolution in sight. As a result of Arendt's subsequent treatise on "the banality of evil", she was again vilified by outspoken members of the international Jewish community as a "self-hating, anti-Semitic Jew". In addition, her ongoing relationship with Heidegger was held forth as clear evidence of that "fact ". Friendships were lost. Any and all criticism of Israel was considered by many to be nothing more than a form of anti-Semitism.

In short, she was deemed guilty of a serious lack of *Ahabath Israel,* (love of the Jewish people). Arendt, who always self-identified as a member of her tribe, replied with another statement about love. "I have never in my life "loved" any people or collective... or anything of that sort. I indeed love only my friends and the only kind of love I know and believe in is the love of persons". (Daniel Maier-Katkin and Nathan Stolzfus, theamericanscholar.org, June 10, 2013).

As Hannah and Martin continued on with their special

relationship, the aging philosopher expressed his wish that since he loved both Hannah and Elfride that his two women should also love each other. This was, of course, not possible, since both of these fierce women were intensely territorial in regards to him and each was determined to prevail as the one and only most important woman in his life. Moreover, the roles of wife and mistress are necessarily quite different. Eventually, these bitter and determined rivals arrived at an uneasy and also necessary truce. Heidegger and Arendt continued to correspond and she visited with the Heideggers during her yearly journeys to Europe. His last letter written to her in July 1975 was warm and caring and expressed his joy in seeing her soon; and she came to see him in mid-August.

Hannah Arendt died of a sudden heart attack in New York in December 1975. The following spring Martin Heidegger died of unknown causes.

JULY

Terminal Beach

"Diamonds are forever but radiation lasts even longer".
(Chautauqua Hunter)

"To destroy your planet's ecosystem for imaginary wealth is highly illogical". (Mr. Spock, **Star Trek** Science Officer)

"In a time of universal deceit, telling the truth is a revolutionary act." (George Orwell)

Runit "Cactus" Dome is leaking and this is not good news. First a bit of background history in order to establish some context for the creation of this environmental time-bomb, located in the Marshall Islands; half-way between Hawaii and Australia in the remote geographic area of Micronesia. Runit is an island on the eastern fringe of the Enewetak coral Atoll, which is a part of the chain of 40 islands surrounding a lagoon measuring some 50 miles in radius. Runit provides the nightmare-at-noon setting for master science-fiction writer, J.G. Ballard's short story "Terminal Beach", where he used environmental catastrophe to evoke transfigured landscapes of the human psyche. (Joe Banks, vice.com, July 29, 2015).

Humans had inhabited this remote atoll since about 1,000 B.C. Spanish explorer Alvaro de Saavedra was the first European explorer to arrive in 1529. Later in 1794, British merchant ships came along, and then this territory became a German colony in 1885. Enewetak was captured by the Imperial Japanese Navy during World War I. In 1944, during the Battle of Enewetak, U.S forces captured the island after a five day amphibious operation and thereafter it remained under U.S. Control and became part of our Pacific Atomic Proving Grounds. (Francis X. Hezel, **The First Taint of Civilization: A History of the Caroline and Marshall Islands in Pre-colonial Days, 1521-1885,** 2000).

Local residents were evacuated (forcibly re-located) from Enewetak after World War I;I and then from 1948 until 1958 forty-three nuclear tests were fired on this atoll. As a consequence of the irradiated debris, including plutonium 239, Runit Island will not be habitable for the next 24,000 years, which is why it was chosen as a site for a 25 foot high, nuclear waste repository. Beginning in 1977, U.S. Service personnel simply scraped off the island's topsoil, mixed it with radioactive slurry from other islands and buried 111,000 cubic yards (85,000 cubic meters) of this deadly poison into an unlined 350 foot (110m) wide atomic blast crater, left by the bomb-blast, code named, "Cactus", 30 feet (9.1m) deep. They sealed this crypt under 358 concrete panels, each supposedly 18 inches (46cm) thick.

In truth, some of these panels were as thin as 12 inches and placed without any internal reinforcement or expansion joints. Officially known as Runit Dome; locals call it: The Tomb. This ominous, unlined structure, completed in 1979, does not even meet the most basic American standards for landfills containing non-toxic household trash. From the air, the vast dome resembles some Sci-Fi or CGI downed and stranded flying saucer, partially sinking into sands which sit upon a coral foundation, severely fractured by numerous nuclear blasts. (Michael B. Gerard, **NY Times,** December 3, 2014).

We now learn that this vast monument to human insanity was never intended to last; and only constructed as a temporary fix until a more permanent solution could be found. Allegations of shortcuts and errors during the construction of this deadly dome include; the mysterious disappearance of up to 19,000 cubic meters of radioactive, seriously "hot" contaminants, destined for the Cactus crater which were reportedly dumped down into the clear sapphire waters of the adjacent lagoon; supposedly to create an artificial reef that was clearly not needed. At present, allegedly substandard Portland Type 2 concrete-cracks, riddle the surface while rising levels of Pacific waves lap along its edges.

According to a 2013 report by the U.S. Department of Energy, underground radioactive waste is leaching out of the crater and the soil around the dome is already more contaminated than its contents. (John Green, **Intelligence: Creating Environments that Protect Human Health,** 2009). Locals, scientists and environmental activists are understandably concerned that a storm-surge, typhoon or other cataclysmic event, brought about by climate-change, terrorist attack, or some other unknown, is likely to tear the weakened concrete panels open, or even inundate the entire island; releasing its lethal contents into the Central

Pacific and far beyond, in view of the fact that the Pacific Ocean covers something like a third of our home world. To date, we know that according to a 2014 study published in Environmental Science and Technology, plutonium isotopes from the Enewetak nuclear tests have been detected in China as far as the Pearl River Estuary in Guangdong province.

A 2013 report commissioned by the U.S. Department of Energy to the Lawrence Livermore National Laboratory, acknowledged that radioactive contaminants are leaching out of the dome; while downplaying any possibility of serious environmental damage or threat to human health. Nevertheless, the DOE said that they were planning to repair some "cosmetic cracks" in order to restore public confidence. By now, if you are reading this, you are probably more than familiar with their predictable litany of bureaucratic spin-glish in regards to matters of radioactive contamination and public safety: low or minimal dosages, (spurious) dilution solution, exposure no more than a banana or dental x-ray... and my personal favorite " We are unaware of any immediate danger at this time". Never mind that hundreds of tons of radioactive materials are emitted every day from Fukushima's three damaged reactors, directly into the same Pacific Ocean, with no end in sight.

At present, Runit Island is uninhabited but receives a steady stream of desperate visitors from neighboring islands searching for scrap-metal to salvage, as well as those seeking to explore and profit from its abundant (hot) fishing grounds. (C. Jose, K. Wall, J.H. Hinzel. UK Guardian, July 3, 2015).

Soon, I imagine that Runit dome will be included on a list of destinations for the growing field of atomic-and-disaster tourism, a relatively new "vacation experience", in which travelers learn about Atomic History as well as the American psyche. Must-have travel accessories would probably include a Geiger-counter... (Hazmat suits optional). More on the atomic aftermath in this region is available in "Bikini Atoll": **Waking to the Sound of Thunder: Trauma and The Human Condition II,** A. St. Just, 2013).

AUGUST

Cousin Jack

This land is barren and broken,
Scarred like the face of the Moon,
Our tongue is no longer spoken
And the towns all around face ruin…
If I tunnel way down to Australia,
Oh, will I ever escape …
I'll leave the country behind, I'm not coming back,
Oh, follow me down, Cousin Jack.
(Cornish folk song lyrics by Steve Knightley)

Hirethek: (n.) Cornish for a homesickness for a home to which you cannot return, a home which maybe never was, the grief for the lost places of your past.

While recently being honored with an invitation to serve on the faculty of the Third Australian Constellation Intensive, (www.constellationintensive.com), in February 2016, in Sydney, Australia I unexpectedly uncovered a long-standing generational family fractal involving home and homesickness. While I am looking forward to my first trip Down Under, an admittedly long swim, and connecting with familiar and new international colleagues, this invitation also prompted me to look deeper into a rather obscure episode in my Cornish family history. Family stories, while sometimes colorful, are admittedly unreliable and can unfold along something like a game of Chinese Whispers which re-iterate upon each re-telling.

In short, it seems that my Grandfather, William John Thomas (b.1873) and his brother Marshman (b.1878), either left or were deported to Australia;

for reasons unknown. Some cousins say that they went in search of employment after the mines closed and other cousins maintain that there was some scandal concerning poaching. Most agree that he worked for a time as a sheep herder until word came that his hometown sweetheart, Ellie, now in America, was pregnant, and the brothers booked passage for the USA. My grandparents married and my great-uncle continued on to California. Given the morality of the times, all of this was kept quite secret; and secrecy is a Cornish value for reasons set forth in my previous "Treasure Map" blog.

My maternal Grandparents bought a small farm in rural New Jersey surrounded by a landscape similar to southern England, and I spent my early childhood years there, together with my war-widowed Mother. By all accounts my Grandmother was always homesick and when my Mother, the youngest of five, was a small child, she took her with her back to St. Just, and Mother grew up there. My Grandmother eventually returned to the farm in New Jersey, and had passed away by the time I arrived. Grandfather had taken her ashes back to St. Just. However, I do remember being taken to meet her four surviving Cornish sisters who had never married and always lived together. As a child, I experienced them as shy and ancient old ladies, smelling of lavender, (who were in reality probably somewhere in their fifties), known to smoke unfiltered cigarettes, despite family disapproval.

All of these great-aunts had served together as nurses in a British field hospital in France during World War I. (The horror and the stench must have been beyond awful). Our brief little visit took place during the 1940's and no one was thinking much about war trauma then, except maybe for a few soldiers. Like my Grandmother, my great-aunts were often homesick, crossed the Atlantic many times, and finally resolved to return home to Cornwall. Mother was also beset by a longing for Cornwall, and barely managed one more adult and prolonged visit. Her consolation she said, was her arrangements to be buried there in the town's Wesleyan cemetery; yet, in the end her husband who was not Cornish, could not agree to such a distant resting place.

While these stories do not seem all that remarkable, given my systemic perspective on family systems and trans-generational trauma, I decided to review this and other aspects of our clan's history within the larger context of what is now known as the Cornish Diaspora. It was within this tribal history, that I felt that there might finally be answers to why so many of our clan have always been uneasy living too far from any scent of the sea; and also a possible source for a mysterious, all pervasive, ill-defined and familiar longing, that was integral to nearly all of my childhood memories. Somehow it was collectively understood that our family "home" was in in Cornwall, in and around the small mining town of St. Just, located along the southwest coast of England.

And so, in looking into the history of the Cornish Diaspora, I hoped to find some understanding of this collective pull to return "home", that was so strong in my maternal Grandmother, her sisters, my Mother; and to a lesser extent, myself. In general, those who work with trauma, understand that a compelling need to return and repeat an experience, often has something to do with an interrupted movement or incomplete response; often involving a shock and/or tragedy and possibly a cover-up. More recently, a study of epigenetics has revealed that biological, (epigenetic) markers, can and do retain ancestral memories. With this in mind, I arrived at the salient question: Who longed to return home to Cornwall and was prevented from doing so ?

Emigration was one of the main factors that shaped Cornwall as it is known today. In each decade from 1861– 1901, the County of Cornwall lost at least 20% of its male population following a decline of the mining industry. In total, the county lost over a quarter of a million people between 1841 and 1901. My Great-Great Grandfather Benjamin Thomas, was among those who left St. Just in search of work in the South African diamond mines; reluctantly leaving behind a wife and eight children. We have his letters from that time; when he wrote home weekly, from the time of his departure from Lisbon in February 1888, until his death in July of that same year.

Benjamin Thomas loved the sea and wrote about his long voyage, the beauty of Madeira and the spotting of whales. However, he didn't go ashore for lack of funds; sailing past the Canaries, across the Equator and on into port in Johannesburg. While the family letters to him are lost, his letters home are filled with responses to their news and his clear affection for his family; adjusting to sleeping alone while missing his wife's "warm back", along with special notes of encouragement and fatherly advice for each of his eight children. Throughout his carefully handwritten correspondence it is painfully evident how difficult the economically necessary separation was from both his wife and children, for him and for them, and how deeply he longed to return, with much needed funds.

One of our family ghost stories maintains that my Great-Great Grandmother, Emma, knew that her husband was dead long before an official letter arrived with the tragic news from the mining company. Down in

South Africa, the local news carried reports of a fatal accident on July 10, 1888 in the De Beer's diamond mine in Kimberley; due to management flaunting safety regulations, which resulted in the death of over 200 workers. (University of Cape Town Judge Papers, B 47, Commission of Inquiry into De Beer's Mining Disaster, August 4,1888).

As a newly shocked and grieving widow, my Great-Great Grandmother Emma never believed that fire story. Sometime afterward, she related. and only to close family, that late one evening, days before that awful letter, she had clearly "seen" her husband trying to warm and dry himself beside their coal stove. Dripping wet, he briefly appeared, to tell her that he was so sorry and that he had drowned in a flooded mine shaft ... and so she already knew.

Cornish people who migrated to various parts of the world were often known as "Cousin Jacks", especially in the mining communities. During the 18th and 19th centuries the Cornish led the world in mining technology and Cornish expertise in hard rock mining was highly valued. This term apparently evolved from a story that these immigrants were often asking for a job for their " Cousin Jack " back home; "Jack", being the most popular name for Cornish boys, christened John. Their diaspora can be found throughout the USA, Canada, New Zealand, South Africa, Latin America and Australia; where they brought along their wrestling competitions, saffron-buns, meat-pasties, brass bands, carols, love of nature, and Wesleyan Methodist chapels.

Since I am soon headed to Australia, I did a bit of research which turned up the fact that Moonta, in South Australia, hosts the largest *Kernewek Lowender* (Cornish Happiness) festival in the world; which attracts tens of thousands of visitors each year. Recent ethnographic studies reveal that something like 4.3 percent of Australians identify as Cornish, which makes them the fourth largest Anglo-Celtic group in Australia; after the English, Irish and Scots ... never mind that the Anglo-Saxon English are not necessarily Celts and we find no mention of the Welsh.

In any event, I am looking forward to this entirely new adventure. And while we are on the subject of Cousin Jack, of the several versions of this Celtic ballad available now on YouTube, one can find Steve Knightley's heartfelt rendition offered at the Cambridge Folk Festival, as well as a performance filmed in Port Isaac Cornwall; (the setting for the delightful BBC series, *Doc Martin*, about contemporary village life in fictional Portwenn). Listening once again to "*Cousin Jack*" with something like my intuitive "third ear", I now wonder if my puzzling homesick meme is something more than personal, to me and my own family clan, or more likely something intrinsic within the wider Cornish collective.

This elusive, often unspoken feeling of homesickness, may even dwell within world-wide emigrant systems in general. A wider question then becomes: to what extent has voluntary or forced emigration shaped our family systems; and influenced our understanding of choice within the tribal loyalties down through the generations and on into our individual lives ?

SEPTEMBER

Separation Consciousness

"Who are all these people?" (Robert C. Koehler)

"*The children of our empires are now coming 'home' to Europe".* (Bert Hellinger)

"*Don't just talk about it. Do something".* (His Holiness,Tenzin Gyatso, the 14th Dalai Lama)

"*Once in a while, an image breaks through the noisy, cluttered global culture and hits people in the heart and not the head".* (Douglas Brinkley, Professor of History, Rice University)

Over the years, during my many visits to the Louvre Museum in Paris, I have paused to marvel at Theodore Gericault's monumental, (5mx7m) terrifying masterpiece, **The Raft of the Medusa,** (1818-1819). As an art historian, I saw this painting as an icon of French Romanticism, depicting the aftermath of the wreck of a poorly navigated French naval frigate, *Medusa,* which ran aground off the west coast of Africa on July 2, 1816.

An international scandal erupted as soon as the

public became aware that as the vessel foundered, the fortunate were off-loaded into life boats and at least 147 of those considered to be less worthy were cast adrift upon a hastily constructed, barely seaworthy, makeshift raft; constructed by the ship's carpenter.

Empathetic outrage ensued, as it became known that all but 15 of those unfortunates, literally cast off because they existed at the lower echelons of society, died from exposure, were killed, eaten, or threw themselves into the sea from despair; during the 13 agonizing days before their chance rescue by the *Argus*. The French government had made no specific effort to rescue the raft. Gericault chose to depict the moment when the remaining survivors spotted an approaching ship in the far distance. By this time, these wretched survivors had endured starvation, dehydration and cannibalism; as deep and terrible waves relentlessly buffeted their partially submerged raft. Societal uproar escalated as the tragedy was determined to have been caused, at least in part, by the blatantly political appointment of an incompetent aristocratic captain who had barely sailed in twenty years.

In the foreground of the painting, a despondent father holds the body of his dead son, and to add to the drama of this tragedy, Gericault foreshortened the scene in such a way that the pallid, prostrate, crazed tangle of dead and dying bodies, appear as if the ocean is about to upend the doomed raft in our direction so that this horrifying mess will shortly be ours, as well.

Now, as a social traumatologist, I view this iconic painting from an entirely new perspective. Here in 2015, I understand Gericault's **Raft of the Medusa** not only as a masterful and ground-breaking depiction of an historical tragedy with profound political implications, but also as a nearly timeless depiction of the shipwrecked everywhere. (Michael Glover, independent.co.uk, February 4, 2011).

The image of this Gericault masterpiece also came to mind in the human tragedy and political scandal surrounding "the Raft of Lampedusa", along with a reminder of the power of such images to impact and shift public opinion. Last October's tragedy off the coast of the Sicilian island of Lampedusa briefly hit the headlines, as some 360 men, women and children drowned in the Mediterranean during a failed night crossing. While this incident drew international attention to the failure of the EU's migration policy, at that time, there was not much impetus for change. (http://pes.cor.europa.eu, February 4, 2014).

Then on September 2nd, 2015, the photo of a lifeless three year old boy named Aylan Kurdi went viral, igniting a global outpouring of outrage and sorrow. This photograph taken by Nilufer Demir shows little Aylan in his long shorts and red tee-shirt, hiked above the waist, exposing his midriff, still wearing his black sneakers, without socks, lying face down in the rocky sand. Soon thereafter, Nilufer spotted his five year older brother Galip, lying close by. Words are only that which reach one part of our brains, and this was exactly the image that was needed to break through the collective silence.

During the past several years of warfare,

displacement and flight, more than 200,000 Syrians have died, with many having suffered horrible deaths in bombings, drone and chemical weapon attacks, while attempting to flee their homeland ... their bodies have been found in trucks, frozen in the snow, and now along the beaches. At present, the number of war ravaged, displaced Syrians has mounted to more than 11 million. (Anne Barnard, Karam Shoumali, NY Times, September 3, 2015).

For an exorbitant fee, smugglers had promised Aylan's father Abdullah Kurdi, a motorboat trip from Turkey to the Greek Island of Kos, which faces Turkey's Aegean coast. Their voyage began at 3 AM and then, at the very last minute, instead of a motorboat, these " bait and switch" criminals provided only a 15 foot rubber dinghy for a group of twenty three desperate migrants. Not long afterward, their flimsy, un-seaworthy, flotation device soon capsized amid high waves, fiercely driven by seasonal *Meltemi* winds, often reaching a height of 15 feet, tossing 12 people out into the sea, along with Mr. Kurdi, his wife and two sons; from the Kurdi family only Abdullah survived. (Justin Wm. Moger,

Washingtonpost.com, September 3, 2015). The Kurdi family had been early on their way toward safety and shelter in Canada where family members were waiting to receive them.

So what can be done ? No more silence, willful ignorance, lies and smooth-over media spins. We've had enough of that, and this globalist-generated, massive, for-profit resource-war, and the resultant human tragedy, is not going to go away any time soon. Conflicts that bring chaos, now spreading across the planet, continue to defy any easy solution; and yet a strong international, grassroots, humanitarian response, might succeed where military interventions, "clandestine aid to rebels", no-fly zones and "non-intervention policies" have utterly failed. Truth is, that in our increasingly inter-connected world, none of this matrix-generated reality is very far away from any of us; anywhere, ever. Never before has John Donne's meditation "No Man is an Island ", rung more true:

Any man's death diminishes me, because I am involved in mankind. Therefore, do not ask for whom the bell tolls. It tolls for thee.

Compassion is needed, and this can provide strong medicine for confronting social issues as well as cultivating and promoting an attitude that *all* others matter. While universal compassion sets a high standard, beyond the reach of most of us, we can nevertheless move in that direction by expanding our circle of caring. The challenge here is being able to overcome our, at least partially biologically-determined and culturally conditioned, "tribal consciousness", which dictates loyalty only to "our own"... Gender, family, race, tribe, class, political-party, flag, religious affiliation and so on.

German physician, Karl-Heinz Rauscher M.D., offers a practical way through which we can transcend our tribal limitations and aspire to a more universal and inclusive heart-based consciousness. He reminds us that, as humans, we are a unit, a large family, and with this basic attitude toward life, we have a chance to solve our current refugee problem and also other major human questions confronting us today; by placing ourselves within the "circle of all".

To be willing to place ourselves within this "circle of

all", is to be willing to give up every devaluation and look at refugees as brothers and sisters... and from this inner attitude alone, our necessary actions will naturally follow. Our lives can become much richer through others, and within the "circle of all" everyone gives what they have, (talents, ideas, money) to the center of the circle for the benefit of all; and in this way, everyone will be enriched.

Dr. Rauscher's recommended exercise is as follows: Take whatever time you need and ask yourself: "Where in the world do I still consider another human being to be a stranger, as someone who does not belong to us? "If you find someone, take him or her into your "circle of all" and by doing so, you are entering into the circle yourself, by giving up devaluation and exclusion. Now, stay within this consciousness throughout your day and observe what is happening within you.
(http://www.dr-rauscher.de).

More Death From the Sky: September 11th Lightning Strikes Mecca

On being Muslim: "*These virtues do not have ineffable meaning but offer a sense of morality...a way to be, and a way to behave, as a member of the human family*". (HM Queen Rania Al Abdullah of the Kingdom of Jordan)

"*When the shouting is over, the grim silence of facts remains*". (Joseph Conrad)

"*We're an empire now and when we act, we create our own reality ... we are history's actors ... and you, all of you, will be left to study what we do*". (Karl Rove, Senior Advisor to George W. Bush Administration)

On September 11th, 2015, during severe weather, a massive construction crane owned by the Bin Laden family, was struck by lightning and crashed through the roof of Saudi Arabia's Great Mosque in Mecca, resulting in large numbers of dead and wounded. While many chose to view this tragedy on this date and at that place, as an unlikely co-incidence, others saw the carnage as divine retribution for September 11th, 2001, allegedly carried out by Muslim terrorists. From my perspective, these viewpoints overlook the admittedly complex dynamics of self-replicating traumas as fractal phenomena. (St. Just, A.: **Trauma: Time, Space and Fractals**, 2012).

During many years as both historian and clinician, I observed that individual and social traumas tend to repeat on the anniversary of other traumas, on something like fractal iterations along a non-linear time line. My first attempt to understand and describe this phenomenon took place in 1989 within an analysis of a combat trauma session done by Peter Levine, using his Somatic Experiencing technique, (originally titled: "A Developmental Approach to Combat Trauma", which we later changed to "Under the Lilac Bush"). Peter's client presented with what he described as "a whole string of things"; patterns of trauma throughout his life, which were all somehow connected. This description brought to mind an image of a string of Chinese firecrackers with their linear arrangement of clusters of potentially combustible material. Wherever along these lines the spark is set, the entire string will ignite. Similarly, one can picture trauma as a potentially explosive event that is one of many, arranged in a linear pattern along the course of a lifetime, and this, I then hypothesized, was something like a "Chinese Firecracker Syndrome". (St. Just, A.: **Relative Balance in an Unstable World,** 2006)

Over time, I realized that while these self-replicating patterns of trauma do exist, the repetitions can also be non-linear as well as trans-generational. Then, as I moved into the field of Social and Global Trauma, it became increasingly clear that while traumas tend to happen on the anniversary of previous traumas; this was also evident on much wider levels as well. In general, it can be observed that many replicating social and global traumas tend to occur on the anniversary of previous social and other collective traumas, especially those involving broken connections and various forms of loss. Politicians, activists, terrorists and the media, know this and they often strive to orchestrate events on an anniversary of overwhelming social and political life-events.

These specifically dated occasions are designed to

bring attention to something unresolved, which often contains elements and various levels of denial, lies and cover-ups. Absence of accountability is also a factor in many patterns which are perpetuated when something, or many things, remain interrupted or otherwise unfinished. On a national scale, Americans would see this manifest in the horrors of September 11th, 2001, which can be seen as both the cause and the result of other cycles of violence.

In **A Question of Balance,** (2008), I explored some of the dates surrounding the now totemic date of September 11th, using biologist Rupert Sheldrake's notion that places have "Fields of Memory", that can also play a role in traumatic repetitions. A series of events which took place on or around that date, now compressed into digital shorthand as 9/11, were immediately blamed on Muslim, mostly Saudi Arabian terrorists and a "clash of civilizations". This perception, laced with religious and messianic overtones, served as justification for a series of unending wars beginning in Afghanistan; followed by a Second Gulf War invasion of Iraq. Since then, war has been the single organizing fact of our society and we now garrison over a thousand military bases in at least 153 countries throughout our globe. And still, the possibility that there could or even should be foreign bases located right here on our own U.S. Soil, remains absolutely unthinkable. American exceptionalism reigns.

September 11th was also the eleventh anniversary of the "New World Order" speech that the former CIA director and then U.S. President, G.H.W. Bush senior made to a joint session of Congress to announce his administration's decision to launch the First Gulf War. It is also interesting to note that the construction of the Pentagon, which was also a target on 9/11, began on September 11th, 1941.

Soon after the 9/11 attack, Internet rumors suggested that September 11th 2001 echoes that date in 1683, of the Battle of Vienna, considered to be a final turning point in the battle of the Christian West and Islamic Ottoman Empire. In September 1697, the Ottoman Turks lost a large amount of East European territory, following another devastating defeat by the Austrians. However, the exact date of these temporal correspondences cannot be altogether certain, since the dates of the Islamic lunar, and western solar Gregorian calendar are not the same.

Another "clash of civilizations", along with the theme of "imperial overreach", began on September 11th, 1906, when Mahatma Gandhi announced his plans for a non-violent resistance to British imperial rule. Then, in Chile, on September 11, 1973, our own American CIA, backed a coup which resulted in the overthrow and controversial death of democratically elected President Salvador Allende. The subsequent fascist regime of General Augusto Pinochet, swiftly launched the terrors of Operation Condor, which resulted in the "disappearances" of thousands of people, domestic surveillance, secret police, and firing squads; while Nazi-style concentration camps and torture chambers opened up throughout Chile, as well as within many other Latin American countries. (John Dinges, **The Condor Years:** 2004).

September eleventh has a tragic resonance in the Middle East as well. On that exact date in 1922, ignoring Arab grief and outrage, the Imperial British government issued a mandate in Palestine which promised European Zionists a national homeland for the Jewish people. This in turn, set the stage for ongoing conflict, terrorist attacks, and wars. Again, on September 11th, 1972, a Palestinian terrorist group named Black September killed eleven Israeli hostages at the Munich Summer Olympic Games, where date, place, and number of victims were part of the message.

Now on September 11th, 2015, the latest iteration of this ongoing fractal appeared when a huge crane owned by the Bin Laden family, deployed to a construction project in Mecca as part of an ambitious project to increase the area of the Masjid al-Haram Mosque; (already the largest in the world), allowing it to accommodate 2.2 million people at a time, became a weapon of massive destruction. During an unexpectedly severe electrical storm, over the the holiest site in all of Islam, massive construction machinery was struck by a bolt of lightning and crashed through the upper floors and roof, along the east side of the sacred structure.

Apparently, an unsecured hook from a massive red and white (German Liebherr Group) mobile crawler crane, began to sway during strong winds and heavy rain; and together with a reported lightning strike, began to move the massive machinery with it until the boom toppled into the great Mosque filled with people preparing for evening prayers. At least 109 devout worshipers were killed and some 238 or more were wounded. Some of the survivors were also killed or wounded during a subsequent stampede which occurred when doors were reportedly locked. (dailymail.uk.co, September 11, 2015).

This kind of storm is rare for that region of the Middle East which is normally dry during this season. Meanwhile, the Holy City was inundated with pilgrims, just days before the start of the annual pilgrimage, as one of Islam's five Pillars of Wisdom requires every able-bodied Muslim to undertake the Hajj pilgrimage at least once in their lifetime; if they have the means to do so. This event which comprises one of the largest religious gatherings in the world, has been plagued by chaotic organization, and a series of disasters and tragic episodes; such as the massive stampede of 2006.

Sadly, this pattern was also to repeat on September 24, 2015, in 40+ degree heat, giving rise to dehydration and exhaustion; as harsh policing and aggressive hordes led to the horrific and deadliest stampede which killed at least 2,411 pilgrims and injured hundreds more in a large valley in Mina, where large crowds carry out a symbolic stoning of the devil; which has also been the site of similar stampedes in years past.

As news of this shocking catastrophe reached the West, and our American mainstream media in particular, the response from many was to view this tragedy with some measure of satisfaction, as some kind of "act of God" in vengeful retribution for the events of 9/11; especially since it took place in the holiest site in Islam and involved machinery owned by the Bin Laden family. One blogger went so far as to suggest that the German crane owned by the Bin Ladens was manufactured from steel from the World

Trade Center and Building Seven rubble, that the U.S. sold to China.

Shortly after posting the initial version of this blog, an email arrived from reader Korhan Tekin, calling attention to close ties between the World Trade Center's architect, Minoru Yamasaki and the Bin Laden and Saudi Royal families. The Japanese-American architect notably practiced an architectural style merging the modern together with Islamic influences. The Saudi Royal's admiration for Yamasaki's design for their King Fahd Dhahran Air Terminal is pictured on one of their banknotes. Just a year after the completion of the Dhahran Airport, Yamasaki was awarded the commission for the WTC, which he conceived of as a kind of "Mecca".

Yamasaki's design sought to replicate the pattern of Mecca's courtyard by creating a vast delineated square with low colonnaded structures, capped by two minaret-like square towers. His courtyard also replicated Mecca's assemblage of holy sites; including the Qa'ba (cube) containing the sacred stone, together with a Holy Spring represented by a fountain within an architectural composition in a radial circular pattern similar to that same configuration in Mecca. At the base of the Twin Towers, Yamasaki employed stylized pointed arches derived from Islamic designs. (Laurie Kerr, Slate.com, December 28, 2011).

Unless you prefer to speculate about some HAARP-engineered, weaponized weather involvement, I have another perspective which might also be worth some serious consideration; especially since these ongoing historical fractals seem to be propelled by lies, cover-ups and denial, together with an ongoing lack of resolution. Along with nearly half of our American population, I do not give any credence to that Orwellian myth of an evil Osama Bin Laden as any kind of cave-dwelling mastermind, who sent Arab boys with box cutters to topple our ever expanding empire.

However, this insidious, socially engineered propaganda has nevertheless persisted as an ongoing "they hate us for our freedom", anti-Islamic meme, which seems to have taken on an energy of its own; something like end- times prophesies... which only serve to foster tribalized warfare and apocalyptic visions of death and destruction. I am now amazed, that these matrix-generated memes, which may or may not have anything to do with actual truth, can actually foster such life-negative fractals as the unfortunate energies surrounding the date of September Eleventh.

If this might even possibly be true, what now? We have many choices, of course, including the option to remain awake, aware and conscious of the powerful forces which are known to benefit from the many levels of skillfully-crafted deception, which have been operational throughout history. From my perspective, any message that incites, promotes or supports "us versus them" divisiveness, should be deeply suspect as not being in the best interest of our much needed human healing and harmony.

While we are living in increasingly dark times, this is not the first time that humanity has faced formidable challenges, and while some maintain that these 21st century days are doomed to be our last, I do not agree. While we still have a measure of choice, we can decide to reject those negative and likely untruthful memes about "them", constantly fostered by a monstrous and manipulative matrix; and return to the deeper truths of a compassionate love which connects us all; to find our collective path toward healing from there. There really is no "them"...and that, in reality, leaves finally and only... just us.

OCTOBER

Outrage of the Month: America's War on Halloween

"*May the forces of evil become confused on the way to your house*". (George Carlin)

"*Humans are nervous, touchy creatures and can be easily offended ... They become focused and energized by taking offense; it makes them feel meaningful and important*". (Michael Leunig)

"*The farther we've gotten from the magic and mystery of our past, the more we've come to need Halloween*". (Paula Curan, **October Dreams**)

"*There are three things I have learned never to discuss with people: religion, politics* and the Great Pumpkin". (Linus Van Pelt, **It's The Great Pumpkin Charlie Brown**)

Perhaps you remember a time when Halloween was a fun- loving little holiday, when folks enjoyed using their imaginations to don costumes, go around the neighborhood trick-or-treating; carve pumpkins, decorate homes, schools commercial buildings and public spaces with spooky themes and harvest-time imagery. Growing up in a Celtic household we understood that this was a time to enjoy caramel light,

Autumn colors, apple bobbing, scary ghost-stories, community bonfires, masquerade balls, and to beware of mischief-making pranksters while visiting haunted attractions.

Halloween, a contraction of All Hallows Eve, is generally known as a celebration on October 31st, observed in a number of countries, that marks the end of harvest season and the beginning of winter. In our Cornish family tradition, Halloween was regarded as a liminal time when the veil between this and other worlds, including the realm of the dead, was especially thin, and an opportunity to connect with our ancestors.

Now, in our increasingly dystopian society, we find that Halloween has joined several other holidays which provide occasion for our ongoing, culture-war flare-ups and petty thought-police, control drama campaigns. Dedicated Christian, Michael Snyder is apparently secure in his belief that Halloween is nothing more than a pagan celebration of dark and dangerous supernatural forces. In a similar vein, he warns that, here in the USA, the number of self-identified witches, coming out of the broom-closet, doubles every 30 months. Moreover, Snyder maintains that for the last eleven years, dressing up as a witch has been the premier costume choice for adults and that there may be as many as 8 million undeclared practitioners of "the craft", throughout our country. (endoftheamericandream.com, October 2015).

To be fair, not all Christian Americans are such tightly wrapped Evangelicals, scared of their own shadow; and a number of other faiths also refuse to celebrate Halloween, for various reasons. Most simply choose to leave the rest of us costumed revelers in peace.

It seems however, that our ultra-conservative, Christian communities remain divided on the subject of Halloween. As part of their ongoing war on sanity, Fox News took this opportunity to promote Halloween as a force for "All American Good" in need of defending against immigrants with cultural differences (mostly Muslims). According to their ongoing noise-machine, the real demons of October 31st, are those schools and communities banning costumes and celebrations out of consideration for outsider induced, political correctness. So, basically, this mainstream media "news" channel is devoting prime time to their message that Halloween fun is being canceled because of the immigrants, who, we are told, are also responsible for climate-change, economic collapse, epidemic diseases and more.

Never mind that Halloween was originally brought to our shores by immigrants.
(Hunter, thedailybeast.com,October 31st, 2015).

Contrary to what one might expect, even our Goth sub-culture has issues with Halloween; that one day of the year when their pale faces, and basic-black wardrobe of vintage elements from another era actually blend in. As I understand, their basic complaint is that, on this one day the "normals" adapt their style, and then revert to ignoring them during the remaining 364 days of the year. (dailybeast.com, October 30, 2015).

While trick-or-treating excursions throughout the neighborhood in search of sweet treats used to be fun and a bit scary, paranoia now reigns. In many communities coercive types have banned this practice due to media -driven scare stories about drug and razor blade laden fruits and candies, despite the reality that verified cases of strangers handing out anything that actually killed kids is practically zero.

Nevertheless, as a parent and grandparent, I support the idea that adult supervision is always advisable and that all candy bags be thoroughly inspected with a necessary   minimum of fear-inducing fuss. Other vague concerns about safety and food allergies have put the kibosh on kids enjoying Halloween treats, and "responsible parents" have taken to posting local notices encouraging people to hand out carrots on Halloween; and they have posted signs urging neighbors to avoid giving treats with nuts, gluten or dairy. As a celiac myself, with multiple allergies, I can understand the care and concern involved with this effort, however, I cannot quite imagine a child overjoyed to return home with a bag full of carrots, or even... apples only. We do need to remember that kids can also choke on carrot sticks and many studies have proven that chocolate is actually beneficial for most of us. (salon.com, October, 29, 2015).

Evidence that the spirit of the Halloween Grinch is

alive and well, appears in schools which prefer to celebrate this holiday as an all inclusive, shadow-denying "Fall Festival". While I am all for inclusive Fall Festivals, I remain uncomfortable with these events being promoted as either inter-changeable or some sort of politically-correct replacement for Halloween. Consider for example, the back-bending policy of elementary schools in Connecticut where students will be permitted to dress up as "literary characters", as long as it is clearly understood that theirs is not a Halloween costume. Within this policy, a Frankenstein outfit is completely acceptable because he is a literary icon. Politically-correct culture, also known as speech and thought control, continues unabated. In everyday reality, this means that talking in any accent other than your own is politically incorrect, during Fall Festival or anytime, ever. (salon.com,10/29/2015) Very challenging news for our late night and stand up, character-driven comedians.

As Katherine Timpf advises, if you dress as a sexy nurse or teacher, it then becomes your fault that they are paid less, and sexy police and female film star costumes, actually make it more difficult for women to succeed in these careers. Black face and Hitler masks are not approved costume choices, nor are head-wraps, hijabs or Saudi burqa or pajamas. Those planning to don fangs or claws should presumably be downsized to within limits approved by local dentists and manicure specialists. With these caveats in mind, my plans to appear as a nudist, while sure to terrify, (me especially, if unauthorized photos surface on Facebook) for reasons other than political, are best postponed for some other lifetime.

If you are still unsure as to how to navigate the complexities involved with our Halloween season, or any closely related night-off for fun, many of our nation's loftier colleges and universities, as long-revered bastions of intelligence and wisdom, have issued fliers with telephone numbers of campus officials, also known as "sensitivity control experts" that those in doubt can consult.

As expected, snarky political or topical news costumes are discouraged, and dressing like someone from another race or culture "carries on a deadly system of oppression". Next we can anticipate legally appointed cultural-sensitivity officers to bust into any location and round up anyone in a sombrero with fake drawn on mustache, Afro wig, or Native American feathers and/or beads. Those already suffering white-knuckle outrage fatigue will have little time to rest, given the predictably absurd culture war skirmishes that will soon be upon us with our upcoming Thanksgiving and Christmas holidays.

Bombs Without Borders: Smoke and Mirrors in Afghanistan

"In war, truth is often the first casualty". (Aeschylus)
"War is peace". (George Orwell, **1984**)

"War in one form or another appeared with the first man... The capacity of human beings to think up new ways of killing one another has proved inexhaustible, as has our capacity to exempt from mercy those who look different or pray to a different God ". (Barack Obama, Nobel Peace Prize Acceptance Speech)

"Violence never brings permanent peace. It solves no social problems. It merely creates new and more complicated ones." (Dr. Martin Luther King)

So, here and now within our increasingly upside down ("war is peace") corporate-owned, media-driven Orwellian world, we learn that one recipient of the Nobel Peace Prize has just bombed another recipient of the very same Nobel Peace Prize; resulting in a disastrous number of causalities, as well as a predictable aftermath of shame, blame and confusion. So far, the basic story is that early Saturday morning on October 3, 2015, US/NATO aircraft unleashed a deadly airstrike on an essential care hospital in

Kunduz, Afghanistan, operated by the humanitarian association, Doctors Without Borders. They are a medical charity, established in 1971 and known internationally in French as *Médecins Sans Frontiers* or by the acronym, MSF.

This volunteer organization is widely known for courage, compassion and their "first in, last out" approach to saving lives and easing the suffering of people caught in acute crises; thereby restoring their ability to rebuild their lives and communities. The Kunduz facility opened with a sign affixed to the front of their compound: "The MSF Trauma Center will prioritize treatment of war wounded and other seriously injured persons without regard to their ethnicity or political affiliations and determined solely by their medical needs. No fee charged." (doctorswithoutborders.org).

On Friday, October 2nd, staff members from their trauma center had climbed up onto the roof of their building in order to lay out a pair of large flags bearing the name of their organization, so that their facility could be identified from the air. Then on a relatively calm night, unseasonably warm for early October, bombing began at 2:19 A.M. This murderous attack continued, in 15 minute waves, for over an hour despite frantic calls to both pre-arranged NATO and Washington contacts, to plead for them to make it stop. The appeals were to no avail, even though MSF had long since given these "authorities" their GPS coordinates, and as a result, their attackers knew very well both the exact nature and location of their medical-surgical trauma hospital established in 2011; the only facility of this kind for the entire province of Northeastern Afghanistan.

Our officially sanctioned bombing attack succeeded in killing at least 42 people; among them medical workers, patients, caretakers and children. Currently, 24 staff and 9 patients are still unaccounted for, so the death toll, euphemistically known as "collateral damage", is likely to rise. (Dave Lindorff, thiscantbehappening.net, October 8, 2015). According to an internal report released by MSF, pilots shot at terrified staff members fleeing their hospital, like cowboys high out on some videogame/shooting range.
(huffingtonpost.com, 11/05/2015)

The first of many of these bombing waves on a building so over-capacity that staff had to place mattresses and pillows in corridors and administrative offices, targeted an intensive care unit. A horrified nurse reported that "patients were burning in their beds", while another hospital worker said that he heard women and children crying out for help while their entire facility was consumed in flames and reduced to charred rubble. This unconscionable aerial atrocity, carried out by, huge, low flying, fixed wing ground-attack AC-130 aircraft nicknamed Azrael, ("Angel of Death" in Arabic and Hebrew) involved not only bombs, but rockets, as well as the deadly spraying of intense fire by low altitude canons, designed to annihilate anything moving within range of a target.

Manufactured by Lockheed Martin and Boeing at a cost of $110 million each; these deadly gunships are specially designed to fly at night and are equipped with infrared sensors, and their crews of 12 or more are outfitted with night-vision goggles. While these aircraft are required to employ both audio and visual records of their attacks, we can only expect that this crucial forensic evidence will disappear into some designated black hole of lost file documents; highly classified in the interest of "national security". (Laura Gottesdiener, alternet.org, November 15, 2015).

Doctors Without Borders won the Nobel Peace Prize in 1999 and then, newly elected U.S. President, Barack Obama, was awarded this same honor in 2009 during the time when he was preparing to expand the war in Afghanistan. In 2015, our American President, who campaigned for "hope and change", unleashed a total of 23,144 bombs upon Muslim countries. (Sputnik, 12.01.2015). While one could surmise that as Commander in Chief of the Joint Armed Forces, who bombed this hospital, Obama could hold the dubious distinction of being the first recipient of the Peace Prize to bomb another recipient of the same award. However, as journalist Dan Sanchez points out, this has actually happened before.

In 1973, Dr. Henry Kissinger was awarded the Nobel Peace Prize, which prompted humorist Tom Lehrer to quip; "Political satire became obsolete when Henry Kissinger was awarded the Nobel Peace Prize".

Perhaps some of you may remember that as U.S. Secretary of State, Kissinger masterminded and reportedly ordered the bombing of Cambodia and Laos, during which hospitals were routinely targeted for B-52 bombing. On another occasion, Red Cross buildings were also targeted for annihilation.

Since then, the Red Cross has also been awarded three Nobel Peace Prizes. Those interested in a thoroughly documented account of Nobel Laureate Kissinger's multiple war crimes and human-rights violations, will find abundant material in the documentary film, **The Trials of Henry Kissinger,** (2002) based upon the 2001 book by Christopher Hitchens; which maintains that Kissinger should be prosecuted for war-crimes against humanity.

For those of us who study social trauma and other historical events and look for patterns that connect apparently random, anomalous, or simply ironic phenomena; Nobel Peace recipients being involved in attacks involving war, as either victims or perpetrators, is not so surprising. Consider, if you will, that the founder of this award, ostensibly established for an "outstanding contribution to peace", was the Swedish industrialist and inventor, Alfred Nobel (1833 - 1896), who was a highly successful global armaments manufacturer.

Further ironies become apparent in the identity of many recipients of this "Peace" Prize. Other than warmongers Obama and Kissinger, there was Yasser Arafat, Shimon Peres, Yitzak Rabin, and Menachem Begin ("war is peace"). Given the apparent criteria to qualify, it should be no surprise that Mohandas Gandhi never became a recipient for this blatantly cynical dubious honor of a Nobel Peace Prize. (Dan Sanchez, activistpost.com, October 6, 2015).

Given the world-wide support and prestige of the MSF, and the horrific imagery and eye-witness accounts which soon went viral on the internet, our U.S. fact-challenged chain of command scrambled to find a way to contain the international outrage. No surprise, therefore, that their resident cabinet of spin-meisters soon came up with at least four shape-shifting and conflicting accounts of what actually happened, (as well as spurious justifications for yet another war-crime against humanity).

While harsh criticism and skepticism continues to surround speculation as to the motivation for what clearly is emerging as a deliberate attack upon an MSF humanitarian facility, targeted for destruction; there remains some credible speculation that MSF has been targeted as especially vocal critics of an impending, secretive and controversial Trans-Pacific-Partnership. The MSF has expressed deep concern as to the potential for increasing the cost of life saving drugs, since this "partnership" would limit access to generic pharmaceuticals and would present an immediate threat to the health of millions. This compassion-based objection placed MSF in direct conflict and opposition to the White House (trans-national), profit-oriented TPP agenda. If their opposition to a trans-national globalist agenda persists we and they may expect their humanitarian facilities will continue to be "accidentally" bombed into flaming rubble and/or these atrocities will be blamed on some convenient enemy du jour.

At this juncture in a still unfolding narrative, we can

expect online conspiracy theorists to speculate that some all- powerful trans-national cabal will pressure MSF into accepting a generous "offer that they can't refuse", in exchange for compromise geared toward either accepting spin or silence, in regard to their accusations that they have been victims of a politically motivated war-crime.

For the rest of us, less complicated and still concerned citizens, we might consider Medea Benjamin's perspective which argues that this Kundoz incident offers an opportunity to reflect upon the fact that this and many other inhumane, violent incidents are an integral part of our endless air wars; raging across an increasing number of supposedly sovereign countries, during 14 years of our U.S. "intervention", fully sanctioned by our supposedly Democratically elected (trans-national, corporate and military controlled), bought and paid for Congress. (Medea Benjamin, opednews, October 8, 2015).

Our "intervention" in Afghanistan now stands unopposed, as the longest war in U.S. History, costing the precious lives and well-being of at least 2,350 of our own service personnel, in addition to the lives and health of thousands of participants from our NATO partners; as well as untold levels of trauma and heartbreak for families and other loved ones, which will likely continue throughout any number of subsequent generations. (epigenetics).

To any sane person, this tragic foreign and far-flung fiasco, initially launched as a result of hysterical and Machiavellian calls for 9/11 vengeance, (based upon seriously dubious pretexts), has cost our American tax payers over a trillion tax dollars, which would have been much more wisely spent in the service of our own crumbling infra-structure and other urgently needed, socially oriented, domestic issues. At this point, I am with Glen Greenwald and his summation of the war crime in Kundoz as follows; "The question is whether that's something we want to continue to tolerate; that our own government is singularly exempt and permitted to commit war crimes?" (CNN, October 8, 2015) Yes, and all in response to the lies of 9/11?

Our late Gonzo-journalist and eccentric cultural critic, Hunter Thompson saw the writing on wall:

The towers are gone, now reduced to bloody rubble, along with all hopes for peace in our lifetime, in the USA or any other country. Make no mistake about it. We are at war now - with somebody - and we will stay at war with that mysterious enemy for the rest of our lives. It will be a religious war, a sort of Christian Jihad, fueled by religious hatred and led by merciless fanatics on both sides. It will be guerrilla warfare on a global scale, with no front lines and no identifiable enemy. (Kingdom of Fear, September 12, 2001)

Gore Vidal also got the message, and I miss him too:

You can't have a war on terrorism because that is not an actual enemy; it is an abstraction. That war will be eternal and pointless... It's not a war... it is a slogan. It's a lie. (UK, Independent, June 23, 2006)

Our enemy isn't terrorism. Our enemy is our need for revenge, our compulsion for evening the score, as if that primitive "an eye for eye", offers some sort of highly evolved spiritual justice. Consider for example, Gandhi's much clearer perspective, "an eye for an eye makes the whole world blind"' (Gary Z. McGee, WakingTimes, November, 18,2015). In short: America's war on terror will not stop because it is, in and of itself terror; and we have become this terror as well... with no end in sight.

Svetlana Alexievich

"To bear witness is an aggressive act. It is born out of refusal to bow to outside pressures to revise or repress experience, a decision to embrace conflict rather than conformity, to endure a lifetime of anger and pain rather than submit to the seductive pull of revision and repression. It's goal is change. It's survivors retain control over their trauma - and they can sometimes force a shift in social and political structures". (Kali Tal, World of Hurt, 1996)

"Not knowing doesn't hurt anyone except those who get hurt because nobody knows". (Eric Fried, Austrian poet)

"There are moments when you just have to walk away and cry". (Lou Angeli)

This year's winner of the Nobel Prize for Literature is Belorussian investigative journalist and non-fiction prose writer, Svetlana Alexievich (b.1948). The Swedish Academy cited the author for inventing "a new kind of literary genre", described as polyphonic writings, a monument to courage and suffering in our time..."a history of emotions, ..a history of the soul... an oral history by excavation". Alexievich, a Russian language writer who has never lived in Russia, was born in Soviet Ukraine and grew up in Soviet Belarus and through her books and her life now offers our world's most profound and eloquent understanding of the post-Soviet societies. (Philip Gourevitch, nytimes.com, October 8, 2015).

Her work has held a special significance for mem, since I began my social trauma education and recovery work in the former USSR in 1992. (St Just, **Relative Balance in an Unstable World,** 2006). I arrived in Russia just six years after a series of explosions destroyed Reactor Building Four, soon followed by a catastrophic meltdown on April 26, 1986, at Ukraine's Chernobyl Nuclear Power Station, standing near the newly built city of Pripyat. According to the data published by Dr. Alexey Yablokov et.al. in **Chernobyl: Consequences of the Catastrophe for People and the Environment,** (New York Academy of Sciences, 2010), the death toll, mostly due to cancer, was in excess of 985,000, which does not include the unborn, stillborn and those who died shortly after birth. It is expected to continue to rise since this remains an ongoing global disaster now compounded by the triple-meltdown of Japan's Fukushima Daiichi reactors. (St. Just, **Trauma: Time, Space and Fractals,** 2012).

Cynical bought-and-paid-for nuclear shills, who continue to insist that nuclear power is a clean, green, cheap and safe alternative to fossil fuels and "global warming", and that "nobody died at Chernobyl ", together with any and all who attempt to minimize the human and environmental consequences of this ongoing nuclear accident, should be required to read Alexievich's **Voices from Chernobyl: An Oral History of a Nuclear Disaster** (2005). During her Nobel lecture she spoke of how in Chernobyl one couldn't see, touch or smell radiation; the world around was both familiar and unfamiliar. As soon as she arrived within the exclusion zone, the author was immediately instructed not to pick any flowers, warned never to sit on any grass nor drink water from any well. Death was everywhere and now posed a very different sort of death. Immersed within this nightmare, she added :

For me the world parted; inside this zone I didn't feel Belorussian, or Russian or Ukrainian, but a representative of a biological species that could be destroyed.

And, while we are on the subject, I would also suggest

that nuclear disaster deniers and disinformation agents be required to view the documentary film "Children of Chernobyl", filmed in Belarus, which is freely available to all through YouTube.com.

In this book focusing upon the Chernobyl disaster, composed of a collage of carefully constructed interviews, Alexievich opens with an account of a newly-wed and newly pregnant woman watching her beloved husband, a firefighter, physically disintegrate in his hastily arranged hospital bed. Doctors maintained that he and his gravely ill comrades had been poisoned by gas ... no one said anything about radiation. He perished, 14 days after the nuclear explosions; she was evacuated and their daughter Natashenka, riddled with multiple birth defects, died soon after birth.

The childless widow was given a two room apartment in Kiev in a building known as Chernobylskaya where people from the Chernobyl station are housed. Some are still working at the crippled power facility although most of the surviving residents struggle with serious diseases, are invalids and prone to sudden-death, whereby without warning they just drop dead.

"I am interested in the little people," she explains, "the little great people,...because suffering expands people." In my books", she continues, "these people tell their own, little histories, and big history is told along the way". (Alison Flood, theguardian.com, December 8, 2015). Another story from her Chernobyl book was adapted for film by Juanita Wilson, as **The Door** (2009), which won many awards including an Academy Award nomination. (YouTube.com) While working on **Voices from Chernobyl,** Alexievich realized that she was actually engaged in writing a fourth volume in a cycle which she now calls "The Red Man"; the Soviet person. This five volume series began with the Great Patriotic War (World War I) and ends with the collapse of the former USSR in 1991. Her fifth and final volume is about the loss of Soviet ideals and the aftermath of state-sponsored terrorism, the gulags and multiple ethnic wars. "We are surrounded by victims", she maintains, "and who did this to them"?

Now engaged in her latest projects involving old age,

dying and love, she has discovered a problem. During her inquiries it seems that older Soviet generations have difficulty talking about themselves since they have had no experience in doing that. If asked about love they would respond about how they built Minsk while inquiries about old age would bring forth stories of hardships during the war, as if they never really had a life of their own.

(Masha Gessen, newyorker.com, October 26, 2015)

NOVEMBER

2015 Paris Attacks

Truth Was Everywhere: A Call To Poets

By Gary Lindorff

We poets take no responsibility

For the forms of civilization;

There are architects

To create the shells we leave behind.

It is our nose for truth

That makes us poets,

A requirement of human evolution

That civilization exploits,

Or straight out denies.

Truth does not build on truth.

Each generation may rightly lay claim to it!

It has to be experienced.

And truth is self-sufficient.

A good life can be built

Around some very simple truths.

Being pushed by the wind,

I once found myself caught up

In a storm of milkweed parachutes,

And truth was everywhere...

Architects are illusionists,

And we're running out of toothpicks and tinsel!

Soon there will be cities built out of smoke

And reflections,

But before that happens

There may come a day

When we sit down to a dinner

Of artificial memories,

Choosing from a menu

Of long forgotten tastes.

I remember a cover

Of a science fiction thriller in the 50s,

Depicting an alien landscape:

In the foreground, a canyon

With the rusty hull

Of a spaceship leaning

Silhouetted on a rise,

And behind that, looming

Mirage-like in the distance,

Great mountainous hives of a super city,

Which, due to its remoteness I guess,

Enhances the incorruptible romance

Of an alien dusk.

There is our future, if we're not careful!

Form, gargantuan, cosmic,

Posing as the last, unbuildable city.

But it's always been there!

Like a screensaver on the inner eye

Of a species that never felt at home,

Showing us what we will look like

When simple truths are gone.

Crisis Actors

"Oh what a tangled web we weave when we practice to deceive." (Sir Walter Scott)

"Deception is everywhere." (James Sanborn)

"A lie can travel halfway around the world before the truth has a chance to get its pants on". (Winston Churchill)

"Because today we live in a society in which spurious realities are manufactured by the media, governments, big corporations, and religious groups, I ask in my writing, what is real? Because, unceasingly, we are bombarded with pseudo-realities manufactured by very sophisticated people using very sophisticated electronic mechanisms." (Philip K. Dick)

False flags and other staged events, organized and promoted as agents for social change, as well as catalysts for various social and political agendas, have been with us since the dawn of civilization. While this is not new information for anyone familiar with world history, the precise means through which these deceptions have been carried out over time, have varied in accordance with specific cultures and the logistical and technological means available, in order to carry out these deceptions. Now, within our 21st century media-generated realities, opportunities for deception abound in ways that most of us born during the previous century could not have imagined.

In the wake of 9/11 and subsequent truther movements, launched by citizens wary of less than credulous official story lines, the awake and aware have become increasingly skeptical of corporate and government controlled, heavily censored, mainstream media-outlets. As a result, factions within our so-called alternative media have gained an increasing following, from those who continue to wonder about what is really going on in our own country and our world overall. In all honesty, I think that it is quite possible that we may never really be able have any truthful answers to such questions, now or even many years from now. In this regard, our era is probably not all that different from that of our predecessors.

So, for now, what we do know is that in order for our modern-day staged-events to work, crisis actors are needed, and amputees are especially valuable for on-site make-up artists to simulate fresh wounds. Whatever one may choose to believe or not believe about false-flags and other staged "terrorist" events, the fact remains that crisis actors are very real. Moreover, these clandestine, thespian operatives, are openly recruited by various government agencies, in conjunction with former and paramilitary organizations.

Much maligned journalist and communications Professor, James Tracy, has dared to raise questions and cast serious doubts as to the authenticity of a number of mass shootings and alleged terrorist events. In his memoryholeblog.com, he has continued to address the reality of crisis actors and their potential roles in national and international media coverage. He cites, for example, the Denver based Visionbox Crisis Actors group which issued a press release on October 31, 2012: "Visionbox Crisis Actors are trained in criminal and victim behavior and bring intense realism to simulated mass casualty incidents in public places ... such as a shopping mall." These actors can play the part of shooters, mall employees, shoppers in malls, media reporters and others rushing to the mall, and in motor vehicles around the mall and so on.

Visionbox voice actors can also play the role of persons calling 911 or posting comments on social media sites such as Facebook or Twitter. In December

2012, Visionbox produced a detailed 73 page syllabus "Social Media in Emergency Management", foregrounding the central role of social media to coordinate and convey a catastrophic event. More of their material is available online at http://crisisactors.org., "Trained Players and Actors Making It Real".

According to Gawker, Halo Corporation, a major military contractor, is now also hiring crisis actors. This California based organization was founded by former Special Operations, National Security and intelligence services personnel. According to their Linkedin profile, "Halo exists to provide safety and security for those in need, and to improve force protection, all aspects of security, humanitarian and disaster response." (Ari Spool, http://knowyourmeme.com, 2013).

The presence of intelligence operatives in these exercises is less than reassuring, given former CIA Director William Casey's February 1981 statement: "We'll know our disinformation program is complete when everything the American public believes is false". (CIA Flashback, truthstreammedia.com, January 13, 2015).

Despite a massive media smear-campaign, not everyone is convinced that Professor Tracy's concerns are without merit. Other independent researchers, such as Sophia Smallstorm and former Florida State Trooper, school principal, and school safety and security expert Wolfgang Halbig, have also raised doubts as to some of the official and mainstream media accounts of a number of mass casualty events. Journalist, peace activist and former U.S. Marine, Bernie Suarez takes these concerns a step farther in maintaining that we are living in an era of crisis actor staged-events and calls for an independent investigative body to penetrate government secrecy; and hold crisis actors responsible for enabling these deceptions. To date, the Facebook page, "Let's Out Crisis Actors" has over 1,000 members. (activistpost.com, December, 13, 2015).

DECEMBER

Our Year of Fear

"No one can terrorize an entire nation unless we are all his accomplices". (Edward R. Murrow, Broadcast Journalist)

"To him who is in fear - everything rustles". (Sophocles)

"Sometimes you get the squirrel and sometimes the squirrel gets you". (K. Storm)

Since this is December already and still, here at year's end, I could find no words for the increasingly disturbing events of 2015, I turned to Ursula Le Guin's wisdom for writers. She refers us to Virginia Woolf, who explained that an image, or an emotion, creates "a wave in the mind", long before it makes words. In writing, she continued, one has to capture this and set this working; which apparently has nothing to do with words...and then as this wave breaks and tumbles into the mind, it finally provides words. (Ursula K. Le Guin, **The Wave in the Mind,** 2004). While I could deeply resonate with her insight, the waves in my own mind were multiple, cumulative and approaching the level of a tsunami in response to an unwelcome, somewhat surreal, increasingly sinister, beyond Orwellian reality.

Truly now, who among the awake and aware would not be at risk of overwhelm in the face of that which human-rights attorney John Whitehead has termed an epidemic of historic proportions. A contagion of fear, being spread like wildfire, has succeeded in turning our communities into populist pitchfork-battlegrounds and setting our loyal American citizens against one another...tragic hallmarks of the post 9/11 reality within which we find ourselves at present. We are being force-fed a daily diet of fear, served up together with toxic doses of vitriol, paranoia, and intolerance; and everywhere one turns, left, right or center, internal and external forces continue successfully to foment distrust and division.

For those willing to see, there exists an ongoing strategy to control the populace through dumb-down, anti-history, limited or banned higher mathematical and science education, continuously hostile to the humanities at the university level; in favor of corporate agendas fostered by those war-mongering, military industrial complexes, of which President Eisenhower warned. Ignorance is and always has been a control tool of the elite.

False flags, staged events, soap-opera trained crisis actors and rampant militarism are becoming near daily fare. Evidence is now overwhelming that an elite totalitarian agenda designed to confound citizenry is a reality; along with campaigns to distract, with media-controlled and complicit "news", and mindless, narcissistic, celebrity- chatter, phantom opponents, and turning local minor disagreements into major conflagrations. We are being maliciously manipulated; and fear and discord are promoted as a covert means of control and suppression, with bizarre apocalyptic scenarios intended to terrify.

While our genuinely patriotic and well-meaning citizens are busy screaming at each other, no notice will likely be taken of a lethal control-matrix, swiftly closing in, until the final, virtual and actual, crushing curtain of the controllers' "us versus them theater" inevitably descends. (John Whitehead, "Does Fear Lead to Fascism? (opednews.com, December 7, 2015). With all due respect to John Whitehead, I would add that, from my perspective, this oppressive control-matrix is a globalist operation, not limited to any one culture, country or continent.

And then, mercifully indeed, my aphasic tsunami gradually receded when the multi-media, fear-porn, noise-machine carried their campaign another bridge too far. Words and my much-needed sense of humor returned when the following story of a terrorist squirrel went viral. While you may be tempted to think that what I am about to relate is fiction, I can assure you that the following events are very real and you can research this for yourselves through the multiple sources available online. The first byline to catch my attention was: "WHAT'S GOING ON? Aggressive 'attack squirrels' are terrorizing small California town". No really, I am not making this one up. (catholic.org, 12/07/2015).

As I understand it, the unvarnished facts have unfolded as follows. Richard Williams 87 and his wife Norma 83 required hospitalization in the wake of a vicious attack by a squirrel that had been terrorizing their Novato, California neighborhood. As they were peacefully attending to routine chores in their garage, the perpetrating squirrel allegedly slipped under the garage door, pounced upon Williams, clawing and scratching his head, arms and legs and repeated the attack every time that it was pulled off, and even smashed his glasses!

Upon hearing William's screams, wielding a broom, Norma hastened to his aid, as this furry missile also landed upon her, and more scratches and cuts ensued. As the battle raged on, Williams was able to grab the critter by the tail, swing it down to the garage floor, and then although briefly stunned, the squirrel managed to escape. A kindly neighbor brought the shocked and wounded couple to the hospital where they received dozens of shots for rabies, tetanus and other rodent borne illnesses. Soon thereafter, photos of the bloodied and duly hospitalized Williams went viral.

And, if such an anomalous incident wasn't harrowing enough, the San Jose Mercury reports that this wasn't the squirrel's first strike. Furthermore, the Marin County Humane Society has warned that this very same gray fox squirrel has been responsible for attacks upon at least eight other citizens during the last three weeks. However, the Marin Society also now reports that this purportedly identified squirrel is now believed to be dead (forensic evidence?). While this official sounding announcement may provide some relief for potentially terrified Marin County residents, the question remains as to why this local story about a few people and a squirrel went viral and was even given prominence in the UK. Daily Mail? ("Beware the killer squirrel": dailymail.co.uk, December 8, 2015).

As it turns out, I was not the only one wondering about this squirrel-fueled media blitz. And while I have compassion for the Williams and anyone else suffering fear and pain for whatever reason, I was also comforted to learn that I was not the only one experiencing more than one flashback to those iconic Monty Python comedy sketches, featuring the ongoing battles between mankind and our fellow creatures. Soon after any number of these Northern

California based squirrel-battle accounts appeared in various local, national and international media outlets; the internet comments sections also went viral, for the most part in a sane and comedic tone that categorically rejected any mass media intimations of any kind of genuine terror, whatsoever.

Some of the more astute internet comments are summarized as follows: the attacker was likely a rodent-American of color (grey) recently radicalized by Muslim nuts, probably by his mate who is also a known member of ACORN, and this is why we need military- grade weapons. Others warned that this latest confirmed terrorist attack augers an oncoming zombie-squirrel apocalypse, and that walls should be immediately erected around all of Marin County, and best to steer clear of Novato altogether. Some opined that this vicious attack was possibly provoked, as some neighbors suggested, when the varmint overheard some inflammatory anti-squirrel rhetoric emanating from the Williams' household.

Nevertheless, the squirrel had his apologists who maintain that this bushy-tailed tree-rat should not give all squirrels and squirrelism a bad name and refer sympathizers to their "squirrel lives matter aps#". Others found some good news in the fact that the much maligned fur-person wasn't seriously injured during the attack, otherwise, his elderly victims could have him jailed for life, without parole.

Here in Arizona there have been no reported squirrel attacks, at least none that I am aware of, and perhaps I am naive, but it still seems relatively safe to enjoy the antics of those furry terrorists cavorting around the Juniper tree outside my office window.

Conclusion

"The Matrix is everywhere ...It is the world that has been pulled over your eyes to blind you from the truth..you have to understand that most of these people are not ready to be unplugged. And, many of them are so inured, so helplessly dependent on the system that they will fight to protect it ". (Morpheus, **The Matrix**)

"One of the saddest lessons in history is this. If we have been bamboozled long enough, we tend to reject evidence of the bamboozle ...no longer interested in truth... The bamboozle has captured us... It's simply too painful to acknowledge, even to ourselves, that we have been taken". (Carl Sagan)

"The challenge that is already with us is the temptation to accept as true freedom what is in reality only a new form of slavery". (Pope John Paul II)

We live in a world of shifting paradigms and it has been recently suggested that we are currently living in what should be now called, the Anthropocene era, given the world changes brought about by our partially domesticated species: Homo sapiens. This new term Anthropocene combines *anthropo* meaning human and the root *cene*, the standard suffix for epoch in geologic time. This suggestion came about in recognition of the fact that, over the past two Centuries, humanity has generated mass extinctions of plant and animal species, poisoned every ocean on our water planet, as well as our atmosphere, while weaponizing other organisms essential to life.

Nevertheless, this newly suggested term has not been universally accepted. According to the International Union of Geological Sciences, we (officially) remain within the Holocene (entirely recent) era which began after the last major ice-age some 11,700 years ago. Yet, according to N.Y. Times reporter Andrew Revkin, it is significant that this issue is being debated at all. As he points out, two billion years ago, cyanobacteria oxygenated the atmosphere, thereby disrupting all life on Earth. Apparently remaining unaware of the impact on their biosphere, Homo sapiens is the first species to become a planet-wide influence, that is also aware of their various planet changing agendas. (Joseph Stromberg, Smithsonian, January , 2013) .

Now, on the cusp of 2016, it seems to me that even more important than a precise nomenclature for the times in which we are living, is a recognition that are moving into a future that is radically different from our remembered past .

For some this is experienced as a rude awakening ... or shock, even ... And for others this has been and still is something like watching photographs develop as their images gradually emerge within a specially constructed, darkened room.

As psychologist and author Mary Pipher (**The Green Boat: Reviving Ourselves in Our Capsized Culture**, 2013) explains her current understanding of the human condition; our common phenomenological state is one of collective overwhelm. (social trauma). We are bombarded with too much information, too many choices and way too much complexity. We have mammalian arousal systems (limbic) and neolithic (reptilian) brains, Medieval institutions, combined with 21st century technology and communication devices. Our biorhythms have become en-trained with soulless machines. We operate in nanosecond fields of time, as we struggle to slow down and relax. No surprise that our culture is making us all, at least a little bit crazy. Yes indeed, I quite agree, and even worse, we have the likelihood that the price of sanity within our own and other dysfunctional societies is a certain level of isolation, exclusion, or worse.

While one could easily or even eventually become disheartened, given the daily and cumulative onslaught of uncertainties and often toxic, polarized, rhetoric; the late Joseph Campbell saw no need for us to disappear into the black holes of avoidance, denial, lies, and cover-ups. As the wise mythologist and university professor made clear, all societies are evil, sorrowful and inequitable; and so they always will be. Therefore, if you really want to help - what you will have to learn and to teach, is how to live in them. And, no one can do that who has not himself learned how to live within the joyful sorrow and sorrowful joy, of the knowledge of life as it is. (**Myths to Live By,** 1993).

Bert Hellinger, German philosopher, theologian and founder of Systemic Constellation Work, said something quite similar in **Acknowledging What Is** (1999). Admittedly, such sage wisdom and apparently pragmatic advice presents no small challenge. And yet, those of us who are willing and able to at least imagine a more compassionate and sustainable world must find a way, individually and also collectively, to discover some imaginative means to live outside of and beyond the all-pervasive lies of the iconic controllers of the ruling, global, plutocracy; and their weapons of mass distraction. And it may well be that at first, that for many of the newly awake and barely aware, only small steps are possible, in order at least to be able to begin to recognize, preserve, and then if necessary, defend, all of that which is and has been important to us. There's lightning on our horizon and as visionary author, Terrance McKenna, (who most certainly knew the score), advised sometime toward the end of his life, "If you don't have a plan, you will surely become part of someone else's plan ".